CONSULTANTS
& ADVISERS

CONSULTANTS & ADVISERS

A best practice
guide to choosing,
using and getting
good value

Harold Lewis

RECOMMENDED BY
INSTITUTE OF DIRECTORS

KOGAN
PAGE

London & Sterling, VA

This book has been endorsed by the Institute of Directors.

The endorsement is given to selected Kogan Page books which the IoD recognizes as being of specific interest to its members and providing them with up-to-date, informative and practical resources for creating business success. Kogan Page books endorsed by the IoD represent the most authoritative guidance available on a wide range of subjects including management, finance, marketing, training and HR.

The views expressed in this book are those of the author and are not necessarily the same as those of the Institute of Directors.

Publisher's note
Every possible effort has been made to ensure that the information contained in this book is accurate at the time of going to press, and the publishers and author cannot accept responsibility for any errors or omissions, however caused. No responsibility for loss or damage occasioned to any person acting, or refraining from action, as a result of the material in this publication can be accepted by the editor, the publisher or the author.

First published in Great Britain and the United States in 2004 by Kogan Page Limited

120 Pentonville Road
London N1 9JN
United Kingdom
www.kogan-page.co.uk

22883 Quicksilver Drive
Sterling VA 20166-2012
USA

© Harold Lewis, 2004

ISBN 0 7494 4136 4

British Library Cataloguing-in-Publication Data

A CIP record for this book is available from the British Library.

Library of Congress Cataloging-in-Publication Data

Lewis, Harold, 1933-
    Consultants and advisers / Harold Lewis.
        p. cm.
    Includes bibliographical references and index.
    ISBN 0-7494-4136-4
    1. Business consultants--Selection and appointment. I. Title.
        HD69.C6L443 2004
        658.4'6--dc22

                                                              2004006664

Typeset by JS Typesetting Ltd, Wellingborough, Northants
Printed and bound in Great Britain by Creative Print and Design (Wales), Ebbw Vale

Contents

List of figures

Preface

Everyone in business will at some time or other need professional help. If your background includes accountancy – and you have kept up to date with changes in tax affairs and so forth – you may feel confident you have the accounting skills needed to run your company. If you have legal qualifications and know your way around company law, you may think you have little cause to consult a lawyer. But even so, there will be occasions when it makes good sense to seek help in dealing with matters outside your competence or in sorting out a difficult problem. If your company is like most businesses, you will have come to regard using accountants and other advisers as a fact of life.

This book guides you through the process of choosing and using consultants so as to secure the help you need and the results you intend. It is directed not just at businesses in general, but also at non-commercial groups and organizations, as well as individuals who have reason to engage professional advisers. If you are a small business or a householder needing to use a consultant, perhaps for the first time, this book is meant for you! Its intention is to help you avoid mistakes and pitfalls, save time, money and effort, and make the process of working with consultants really worthwhile.

There may be lessons in its pages even for big companies and corporate organizations. It is surprising how frequently clients whom one would expect to be shrewd about these matters get their fingers burnt. Where levels of risk are high, poor advice can cause financial loss and at worst put firms out of business.

Chapter 1 identifies the kinds of situation in which professional help may be necessary or useful, discusses various ways to obtain this help and indicates circumstances in which bringing in outside advisers may not be the best course of action. Chapter 2 offers a profile of the consultancy and professional services sector, describing the basis on which consultants work and offering an insight into the way they view relationships with their clients. Consultants' fees and expenses are analysed in Chapter 3. The points to take into account in deciding your requirements, planning the work and developing a work specification are examined in Chapter 4.

Chapter 5 explains step by step the process of selecting the consultant who is right for you, from initial contacts and interviews to determining the 'best buy' proposal. Chapter 6 provides advice on drawing up contracts and negotiating with consultants. How to keep track of the work and get it back on course if things go wrong is the subject of Chapter 7.

Though the book does not address directly the use of consultancy services by public sector clients, since they have access to a fund of guidance from government, the factors that differentiate public sector procurement in the UK from general business practice are significant, and they are outlined in Chapter 8. The book concludes by considering ways to obtain best value from consultants and the factors conducive to successful client–consultant relationships (Chapter 9).

Several case studies illustrate aspects of the client–consultant relationship, as well as offering pictures of good and bad practice in action. There are also personal viewpoints in which people from various professional and business sectors comment first-hand about their experience of consultants and offer pointers that it is hoped will be particularly helpful to new and less experienced clients.

The book includes numerous figures, many of which are intended to exemplify ways of treating their subjects rather than necessarily serving as models. To avoid breaking the flow of the text unduly, lengthier figures such as examples of contracts have been placed at the end of chapters.

There are points of terminology that need to be made clear at the start. Professional services embrace a huge array of skills and competencies. In most areas of practice people refer to themselves as consultants; in others, such as accountancy and law, it is usual to talk about advisers. Throughout this book the term 'consultants' should be understood to include advisers and anyone else providing expert guidance professionally. For the sake of consistency, the plural term 'consultants' is used in most parts of the text rather than the singular 'consultant', but the term is meant to cover individual practitioners as well as consultancy firms. As someone who is himself an independent consultant, the author intends no bias against persons in business on their own!

Acknowledgements

I am grateful to my friends and colleagues Peter Downs, John Partridge and Jeremy Seldon, who read sections of the manuscript in its advanced stage and made many suggestions that helped to clarify and improve the text. Any errors and omissions in the text are, of course, entirely my own responsibility.

I need to thank those individuals who contributed viewpoint material and kindly gave permission for me to use extracts from articles and other publications. My thanks are due also to Peter Coysten, who helped with some of the contract material included as examples, Chris Sheridan of the Royal Town Planning Institute, and Jon Finch, Commissioning Editor at Kogan Page, for his encouragement and guidance.

1

Why would I want to use consultants?

THIS IS WHAT CLIENTS SAY

When business managers are asked why they use consultants, their replies typically point to three factors (Figure 1.1):

- the expertise that consultants offer;
- their independent viewpoint;
- the resources they provide.

Expertise

- 'We're able to tap into skills and knowledge outside the competence of our own staff.'

- 'Because they are specialists in their field they focus directly on the work. That means they get results more efficiently than we could ourselves.'

- 'We faced a difficult business situation we hadn't met before, and were unsure what to do. But it was something our management consultants had seen in a lot of other firms, and they knew the pros and cons of different approaches. We had the benefit of their broad experience.'

- 'In restructuring the firm, we had tried to sort things out for ourselves, but seemed to get nowhere. They saw we had been asking the wrong questions, and helped us get to the root of the problem. In the end we did find our own solution, but it was with their help.'

- 'We knew the business had to change, and we saw where we wanted to go; but we didn't know the best way to get there.'

- 'The risks of making the wrong decisions about equipment and supplies were so enormous, we had to get informed advice from experts.'

- 'We had become set in our ways and needed a new vision to get us moving. The consultants played a key role in facilitating changes in our thinking and motivating our team.'

- 'They gave us an awareness of best practice across the computer industry. We were able to stop wasting time inventing wheels that had already been designed elsewhere.'

- 'Working alongside our people, they can help sharpen up our skills in specialist areas. There is a definite transfer of knowledge that takes place, and this is one way they add value to our business.'

- 'What we get are ideas we might not have thought of ourselves. I suppose you could call it lateral thinking or thinking out of the square or just creativity. They're often ideas that can help us cut costs and bring in new income, ideas that hopefully will build up our business advantage.'

- 'Technologies move fast in the renewable energy sector. Our consultants keep us up to speed with new processes and new areas of development.'

Expertise	Independence	Resources
Specialist skills	Detached viewpoint	Outsourcing
External competencies	Impartiality	Meeting workload pressures
Breadth of experience	Unbiased analysis	Freeing up management time
Depth of insight	Bridge between interests	
Focus and direction	Professional judgement as technical collateral	Fulfilling management roles
Awareness of best practice		Cost-effective response to occasional or short-term needs
Facilitating change	Legal requirement for independent advice	
Identifying and diagnosing problems		Opportunity for cost savings
Adding value through knowledge transfer		
Lateral thinking		
Creativity and new ideas		
Access to research data		

Figure 1.1 _Some reasons for using consultants_

- 'To meet the requirements of our own clients, we needed to have quality accreditation. Specialist consultants guided us successfully through the procedure.'

- 'Putting in planning applications, lodging appeals and acting for us in planning inquiries – these are areas where we need expert advice.'

- 'We needed to obtain an environmental resource consent at an early stage in a development project. We were not sure what information we would have to provide, but our environmental consultants had been through the process many times before and they helped us submit a successful application.'

- 'We were impressed by the range of market research data the consultants had available. We would otherwise not have had access to that information.'

Independent viewpoint

- 'Sometimes we're too close to a problem to see it in its true perspective, and we miss points that are obvious to everyone else.

3

Consultants can help us think situations through and challenge the way we go about things. Looking in from outside, they can identify what we need to do to improve our business performance and service delivery.'

■ 'They can take a more objective and impartial view of a situation than we can. They don't bring with them any baggage of management self-interest.'

■ 'Our relocation plans at times involve contentious issues and feelings run high. By using consultants we can obtain a neutral and dispassionate analysis of the options.'

■ 'There is a valuable role that consultants can play in acting as a bridge between different and perhaps conflicting interests, a line of communication that doesn't wear the label of one side or the other. People will speak more openly to them than they would to us.'

■ 'Investors are unlikely to fund a project unless it has had its feasibility checked independently. So a consultant's judgement that a project can deliver an adequate return is an essential form of technical collateral.'

■ 'Apart from due diligence concerns, our work on pension and investment schemes has to involve independent advisers: it's a legal requirement.'

Resources

■ 'Because of recent cuts, the pressures on our remaining staff have become particularly intense. We are so fully stretched on day-to-day work, we really cannot respond to sudden demands or unexpected problems. That is where consultants come in: they keep our workload afloat.'

■ 'They free up our management to focus on strategic questions.'

■ 'We have sometimes brought in consultants to fill management positions when things are too urgent to go through a recruitment process.'

■ 'It is management policy: if an activity is not thought central to our operations it has to be outsourced.'

- 'I'm responsible for so much, I am just not able to focus full time on a single project at the cost of everything else. It makes better sense to call in consultants who can give it proper attention.'

- 'It is more cost-effective to use a consultant for work that is short-term, specialized and occasional than to keep an expert on the payroll.'

- 'We save money by using consultants. They will generally work for less, especially if their contract offers continuity, and we're not saddled with the benefit costs of employees.'

CONSULTANTS AND EMPLOYEES

There may be a wide gulf between the type of person you would engage for their specialist expertise or independent viewpoint and the type of person you would contract as a resource to meet a routine work requirement, yet the word 'consultant' is often used in a way that covers both categories. Similarly, some clients apply the term 'contractor' to any individual or firm that signs a contract with them for whatever reason.

The boundary between an individual consultant or contractor and an employee may be indistinct in some work environments. The difference is a material one when it comes to matters of taxation and employment law. Tax authorities may choose to look closely at the terms of contract for an individual's services in case employment is being disguised as a form of consultancy or contracting, with a consequent loss of tax revenue. If the evidence indicates an attempt to evade tax, both the client and the contractor can suffer penalties. As a guide, Figure 1.2 outlines the rules that are normally applied in judging whether a contract involves employment or a consultancy relationship.

Proceed with caution if you are a business proposing to bring in as a consultant someone who left your employment only recently, particularly when the person is to work full time with your organization on the same conditions as your employees and through a service company. In the UK, the Inland Revenue will almost certainly regard that as disguised employment and the person will be required to calculate income tax and national insurance payments on total income just as if he or she were directly employed. Recent changes in the UK tax regime have complicated this issue, particularly with reference to businesses

Degree of management supervision and control		
Is the person...	**Yes response suggests**	**No response suggests**
Able to assign the work to an assistant or an equally competent substitute?	C	E
Required to work set hours, eg 9 to 5 each day?	E	C
Required to work on the client's premises?	E	C
Required to follow a method of work defined by the client?	E	C
Engaged to work on a continuous basis?	E	C
Engaged to produce a specific item of work or deliver a specific output?	C	E
Responsible for operational and management decisions within the client's business?	E	C
Required to submit timesheets to the client, eg on a weekly basis?	E	C
Business status		
Does the person...	**Yes response suggests**	**No response suggests**
Have a contract that describes him or her as an independent contractor?	C	E
Have other clients who use him or her as an independent contractor?	C	E
Have his or her own office or place of work?	C	E
Advertise and market his or her own professional services?	C	E
Submit an invoice for the work on completion of a project or on delivery of a specific output?	C	E
Take responsibility for dealing with his or her own tax and statutory insurance contributions?	C	E
Maintain his or her own liability and professional indemnity insurance cover?	C	E
Receive benefits such as paid leave?	E	C
Run the risk of personally making a loss on the work?	C	E

C Independent consultant or contractor
E Employee

Figure 1.2 *How to tell a consultant or contractor from an employee*

that the Inland Revenue terms 'close companies', broadly companies that have fewer than five directors or shareholders and that pay small salaries and high dividends. An accountant's advice is essential in determining the implications of these measures. Businesses that are aware of the situation need to take care that the way in which they use consultancy services does not prejudice the independent status of their consultants. Later in the book, Figures 6.3 and 6.4 show examples of contracts worded with an eye to safeguarding this independent status.

WHAT ARE THE ALTERNATIVES TO AN EXTERNAL CONSULTANT?

Reading the comments from clients at the start of this chapter, you can see that many of them believed a do-it-yourself approach to the work they needed was not an option. But before you start the process of bringing in a consultant, it is worth considering whether seeking outside help is really the right answer. The root cause of a problem may be a matter of your own way of thinking or the attitudes of the people you work with. If you can look at the situation objectively enough to identify your own shortcomings, you may be able to put matters right by yourself.

Where an independent viewpoint is not the prime consideration, and your organization has in-house staff, could additional training provide the necessary skills? The work may be something that **your own personnel** are perfectly able to undertake, if the time and means are made available. Or perhaps you could call on someone from another part of the business to supply the required expertise or to fill a resource gap. Non-executive members of the board of a company may be in a position to provide a useful form of unpaid consultancy, particularly if they have a broad and varied background of business experience against which to view issues.

Internal consultants are likely to cost less than consultants brought in from outside. They will have good contacts within line management as well as the immediate advantage of knowing the management style of the organization, how it operates and who the key decision makers are; and they may find it easier than an external consultant to win the support and commitment of staff. On the other hand, their range of experience may be relatively limited; they too may be distracted by other responsibilities; and because they are part of the client organization they may not be able to see the situation from a sufficiently detached standpoint.

It may be worth approaching a **sister organization**, an **umbrella body** in the voluntary sector, a firm that is a **business partner**, a **professional institution**, a **trade association** or a local **chamber of commerce** to see if they can offer advice and assistance. Small and medium-size enterprises may find that the consultancy, business counselling and support services offered by **government agencies** such as the Small Business Service (www.businesslink.gov.uk) in the UK and the Small Business Administration (www.sba.gov) and SCORE (www.score.org) in the United States can give them the help they need. Some **professional bodies** run free, voluntary services that provide independent advice and assistance: they are aimed at individuals, community groups and other voluntary groups that cannot afford to pay fees for consultancy.

University and college departments, beside acting in many instances as fully fledged consultancies (Chapter 2), often run management programmes and forums as a means of strengthening their ties with the local business community, and these may provide a source of informal advice.

Most community groups will be able to count on a network of **volunteer advisers** whose knowledge and experience can be called upon in key fields of expertise. Someone on your committee or a supporter of your organization may have just the competencies you are looking for – and with sufficient energy and commitment, people can take on the role of unpaid consultants with remarkable success.

'We had the skills'

Five years ago, Carol Dickinson had just begun to show interest in what the community association was doing on her estate. . . Now she is a member of the consultancy team, as well as holding a seat on the Government's community forum. 'I learnt you don't have to be Brain of Britain or a Mastermind champion to do many of the jobs that would normally go out to consultants', says Dickinson, 38 and a mother of two. 'I am now involved in overseeing both community elections and market research. In the past, there would be a huge financial outlay that would see private companies benefit. That's no longer the case since we realized we had the skills needed to do the job.'

Liverpool Kensington chief executive Steven Boyle says: 'We are going to compile a register of community consultants from the community itself. We have former planners living in the area and many people qualified and skilled in youth and community work. There is a cross-section of skills here and it would be a tragic waste if these were not harnessed for the benefit of the individuals and the benefit of the community.'

(Source: 'Field Experts', article by Paul Humphries in Society Guardian (_Guardian_), 10 April 2002)

Another alternative is the help available on **Internet** topic forums, discussion groups and bulletin boards. It may be tempting to dismiss the Web as a source of advice, but have you ever had a piece of software misbehave, found you couldn't sort it out for yourself, logged into an Internet troubleshooting forum and discovered that someone else had encountered the problem and worked out a solution that you were then able to apply successfully? Of course, you could have paid a computer consultant to produce the same result. As you would expect, material of varying quality and reliability is available on almost every conceivable topic. Anyone can put up a Web site where anecdotage and opinion are passed off as research and where ideas are routinely plagiarized; but there are circumstances in which you may want to use the Internet at least to sound out people's views on a situation or to have the benefit of their experience.

In deciding if one of these alternative routes might be adequate, there are several factors to take into account:

■ the outputs you want to achieve;

■ the scale, urgency and resource implications of the work;

■ the risks and consequences of getting things wrong;

■ the degree to which each alternative reflects a competent professional response;

■ and – if you are thinking of using internal consultants – the qualities and capabilities of the individuals who would do the work.

STARTING THE RELATIONSHIP

When you bring in consultants you are entering a professional relationship. The key purpose of this relationship is to achieve as satisfactorily as possible the results that you want to obtain from the work. Since you own the work, you own the relationship too. Its success will depend largely on how much time and effort you can invest in guiding the work along and the degree to which you perceive the consultants as delivering value. It should not be a passive or compliant relationship on your part. You cannot afford to see time and money wasted through errors or inefficiency.

You may yourself be a consultant or have been one at a previous stage in your career, or you may be accustomed to working with consultants. If so, you will have a good idea of what it takes to make the relationship succeed. The key requirements are confidence, honesty and trust, based on a shared understanding of professionalism and the importance of businesslike delivery. To quote Charles Handy, 'If you trust people, they will surprise you. And they will surprise you positively if their interests coincide with your interests.' You may not know each other well enough at the start to set off on this footing, but it needs to be built up on both sides so as to turn the relationship into a working partnership.

Implicit in this relationship is an expectation that you will allow the consultants to get on with the work without trying to nudge their judgement toward a particular point of view or a preferred answer. The advice you receive may not be entirely to your liking and their findings may tell you things you would rather not hear. But if they are good consultants, they are probably right and it will be in your best interests to take note of what they say. Equally, there should be an understanding that the consultants will view your situation objectively and not try to skew their analysis round to a standardized model or an imported solution that happens to be fashionable in their offices.

As observed in Chapter 2, consultants may go to great lengths to generate the kinds of relationship they believe will encourage clients to choose them in the first place and then to stay with them over the long term. Clients are not always aware of these processes. They might in some instances be surprised to learn how intensively their activities and business plans are analysed by their consultants.

WHEN NOT TO USE CONSULTANTS

'I know something needs to be done, but I'm not sure what.' Fine, this is a question that consultants can help you sort out, and it's a common starting point for many types of work. At least, you're setting out with an objective. But to bring in consultants without any clear idea of the help you want from them is a waste of time and money – you are simply not in a position to place your order sensibly. It is not enough to have them around you just to give you a feeling of comfort and reassurance. There needs to be a specific task for them to fulfil.

You should hesitate also if your past relationships with consultants have consistently ended in failure or yielded far less of a return on investment than they seemed to promise. Perhaps there are problems inherent in the way you approach their involvement, in the way you define (or fail to define) their brief or in your attitude toward them as professionals. Ask yourself where you might be going wrong before risking another expensive mistake.

Projects can also fail in situations where clients are only too well aware of their motives and intentions but choose to use consultants for the wrong reasons:

- requiring them to achieve a result that depends on factors and decisions outside their control: for example, it would not be reasonable to ask a consultant to guarantee that your business wins a contract or that your managing director is interviewed on TV, whereas engaging a consultant to help your business prepare its bid for the contract or to strengthen its relations with people in the media would be reasonable;

- buying their name to give a veneer of credibility to a project known to be unfeasible or a plan that is deeply flawed;

- using them as scapegoats to take the blame for unpopular or disagreeable actions;

- asking them to assume risks that are properly your responsibility;

- imagining they are miracle workers who can solve all your problems;

- hoping they will wave a magic wand over your organization and turn your staff into successful managers overnight;

- wanting them to graft on to your organization attitudes and values that really need to grow from within;

11

- expecting them to arbitrate in deep-seated technical and management conflicts;
- believing they can save you the trouble of defining policies and
  objectives.

These are all recipes for disappointment.

Consultants generally will not be prepared to make statements that run counter to their judgement or support positions they know are wrong. If you were to ask them to do that, you'd be asking them to act unprofessionally. Hire a publicist instead.

BRINGING PEOPLE ONSIDE

The word 'client' is normally understood to mean the person or organization commissioning the work. But the term can give the impression that there is a single person involved in decisions about engaging consultants and a single mind guiding the process. This may well be true if you are taking on consultants in a personal capacity, but in most businesses there will be other managers and decision makers on whom the work will have an impact and whose support may be essential to success. Organizations in the wider community may consider themselves stakeholders in the work, and they can have useful contributions to make to its planning and performance. It is important to discuss the objectives of the consultancy assignment as early as possible with all these interests and get them to buy into it as a worthwhile endeavour.

When the work is being funded by a bank or some other financing institution, this too will become part of the client group. Banks may want to involve their own consultants in the work, and they will often seek to assume the dominant role in the client group as a condition of funding. You will not need to be reminded that their priorities may well be different from yours, and these differences may lead to tensions that put your business objectives at risk. Be alert to this possibility and try your best to ensure that the work is steered on a course that achieves the results you intend.

If your organization has employees and you decide to bring in external consultants, let staff know about your intentions – preferably by talking to them in person rather than sending e-mails – and explain what the consultants have been asked to do, what logistical support they may require and how they are likely to interact with staff members. You cannot afford to have a situation develop in which staff are uncooperative because they feel they are being kept in the dark or fear that their jobs are threatened. Talk to them about the consultants' role in a way that does not suggest you have lost confidence in the abilities of your employees. You need to get them on your side so as to view the consultancy as a team effort in which their participation is important.

MAKING A BUSINESS CASE

People who work in a corporate environment may be required to justify to their organizations the use of consultants, perhaps through the submission of a formal business case. This requirement often applies when the value of the work is expected to exceed a defined threshold and where the risks associated with a business decision call for thoughtful analysis. The business case will normally set out the following information:

- the purpose and scope of the work;

- the results and outputs expected from the consultants;

- the proposed contract basis;

- the estimated costs of the work;

- its proposed timetable;

- the benefits to be derived from the work and when these are likely to be achieved;

- the possible risks arising from the use of consultants;

- the proposed arrangements for managing the work;

- an assessment of the alternatives to the use of consultants – including confirmation that the skills or services required are not available either in-house or from a less expensive source than consultants;

- an indication of how the results of the consultants' work will be implemented.

Managers then have to judge whether the use of consultants is likely to provide a sufficient return on investment.

Using a consultant – a cautionary tale

A farmer whose sheep were dying took his problem to an agricultural consultant. The consultant asked if the sheep were eating long grass.

'Yes, I believe they are,' said the farmer.

'There's your mistake,' said the consultant. 'Make sure they eat only short grass.'

The farmer went away and followed the advice, but another sheep died.

The farmer returned to the consultant who asked if the sheep were standing up or lying down when they ate. When told they sometimes lay down to eat, he advised that they should always be made to eat standing up. The farmer went away and acted on this advice, but two more sheep died.

The process was repeated several more times: 'the sheep should face north when eating', 'they should not eat before six in the morning', 'they should not eat if the sky is overcast' and so forth. Finally the one surviving sheep died.

The farmer returned to the consultant and told him that despite all his advice the last sheep was dead and he would not be coming back again.

'That's a pity,' said the consultant. 'I had so much more guidance to give you.'

(Reproduced and adapted from *Project Management Manual*, Department for European Integration, Government of Romania)

2

How do consultants operate?

PROFILE OF THE CONSULTANCY SECTOR

- The latest survey data available from the UK Office for National Statistics and other information sources suggest that in 2002 over 400,000 enterprises in the UK were engaged in consultancy and professional services.

- Consultants span the whole range of business structures and sizes – from individuals working on their own at home to large companies with corporate headquarters, offices worldwide and thousands of consultant personnel. In most countries the majority of organizations offering consultancy and professional services are small and medium-size enterprises employing fewer than 100 staff.

- In addition to firms that are first and foremost consultancies, there is a huge array of other organizations that provide consultancy and advisory services as part of a broad portfolio of activities. These include university departments, research agencies, business schools and scientific, educational, cultural and commercial enterprises of all types, from training organizations, computer specialists, libraries and archiving services to museums and galleries, sports organizations, broadcasting companies and newspapers.

■ Consultancy and professional advice may be the sole or principal activity of an individual or an organization, or it may be just one of several areas of activity. Work may be obtained through a direct commission from a client, through networking with other consultants or strategic alliance partners, or through a subcontracting relationship with another individual or organization.

■ Organizations that gain their livelihood from consultancy normally work on the same commercial footing as other businesses. Some consulting firms are non-profit – or more correctly, non-profit distributing – organizations. Some are registered charities; but few are in the business of dispensing free advice. In pursuing opportunities for work, consultants will generally be prepared to spend time discussing your situation without cost or commitment on your part. This does not mean, though, that they would be content to let you exploit them by sounding out their opinions and profiting from their expertise without offering any genuine prospect of remuneration.

■ The basis on which consultants are paid for their services is outlined in Chapter 3. Most of their work is in the form of one-off assignments, in which they are contracted to undertake a specific piece of work for an agreed fee. If their work is successful, clients are likely to want to use them again, so repeat business is an important part of their activity.

■ Clients who make regular use of consultants may set up framework agreements with them, calling on their services as and when required (Chapter 6). In sectors of activity that are strategically important to a business, relationships with consultants may extend into long-term partnering arrangements, analogous to buyer–supplier relationships in industry and commerce (Chapter 9).

■ A small firm based in a small town will not necessarily have only local clients or operate only within its immediate region. It would be a mistake to assume that it must have limited skills or the capacity to undertake no more than small-scale work. In contrast, the largest firms with their national or worldwide networks of offices may appear remote and impersonal, but may be able to offer small teams customized to the needs of individual clients.

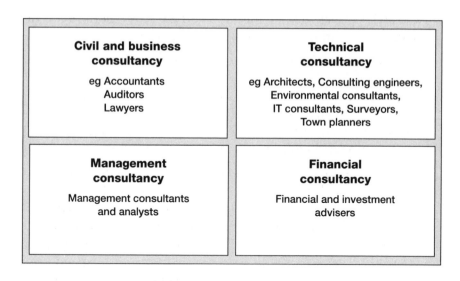

Figure 2.1 _Categories of consultancy and advisory services_

- Consultants may choose to specialize in a particular field of expertise or to offer skills and services in various fields. As a generalization, high levels of specialization tend to be associated with individuals and small firms; it is normally large firms that offer a broad spectrum of expertise, though their personnel may include individuals and teams focused on specific areas of consultancy.

- Figure 2.1 offers a broad categorization of consultancy and advisory services, with examples of the types of professionals working in each sector. Civil and business consultancy covers fields of expertise to which businesses and other organizations will normally have recourse and on which individuals too may need to call. Technical consultancy includes an immense range of specializations, many of which involve the analysis of problems, the development and application of solutions and the delivery of projects. Management consultancy is generally related more to business processes such as achieving structural change, improving organizational effectiveness and strategy alignment than to particular projects, but its products may be just as tangible as those obtained from technical consultancy.

- Some firms are in effect single-issue consultancies, working within a narrow area of specialization and espousing a particular social, environmental or technological perspective in ways that may call into question their impartiality and objectivity.

- Over the past 20 years or so an increasing number of long-established UK consultancies have been bought out or absorbed by larger consulting and contracting firms based overseas. Changes in ownership generally bring with them changes in the management style of the consultancy and its business approach. As a client you may be comfortable with these changes, but you would be well advised to make sure you know who are the actual owners of a consultancy – are they the principals you see in its office or the members of a board that meets thousands of miles away?

- Consultants are considered in law to owe a duty of care to their clients. This means that they have a responsibility to take all reasonable steps to protect their clients from risks that might arise as a result of the way they perform their work.

- The best firms of consultants are committed to improving continuously the services on which their reputation for professionalism is built, while at the same time searching for innovative methods that can reduce the costs of their services and meet the needs of their clients more effectively.

- Not all consultants have to work such long hours as the individual whose diary is shown in Figure 2.2. But then he is in charge of a sizeable project and has management and business development responsibilities within his firm as well as contributing to the activities of his professional institution. On the day in question he can put in only about three hours of fee-earning time. This reflects a pattern that is the norm in consultancy firms. As people take on management roles, the proportion of their time that can be spent on chargeable work reduces, while their salary levels in the firm rise. The implications for the fees that clients are asked to pay are noted in Chapter 3.

- Though the size of a firm may not always be significant when selecting consultants (Chapter 5), some businesses find that in general they get the best quality of response from firms that match their own size and scale of operations. Think of the factors you would consider in choosing an accountant. If you are a small business, you are likely to find that your affairs can be handled quite adequately by a small local firm of accountants or perhaps an accountant working on his or her own – you should be able to count on a helpful degree of personal attention and the costs should be reasonable. Of course, a bigger firm of accountants with a team

7.00...	Breakfast, then work on paper for professional journal.
8.00	Leave home for office.
8.30	Arrive in office – check through day's agenda, confirm meetings, check on status of proposal and report production, read through proposal draft left on desk, suggest amendments and additional material.
9.30	Discuss proposal amendments with team and accountant. Discuss situation with bank: have payments cleared?
10.30	Leave for Richmond office.
11.00...	Progress meeting with Richmond team plus team personnel matters.
12.00	Call in at offices of prospective associates.
12.30...	Lunch with associates.
13.30	Back to office.
14.00...	Work on project.
15.30	Leave for meetings at client headquarters.
16.00...	In business meetings.
18.00...	Panel meeting at professional institution.
19.30	Call back at office: collect draft text of proposal + technical material on project and papers from accountant.
20.00...	Back home.
21.30	Phone colleagues about day's outcomes.
22.00...	Work on papers for Board meeting.

Figure 2.2 *A consultant's day*

dedicated to small businesses may offer a level of service at least as good, together with a greater breadth of expertise, but you would have to pay rather more. If on the other hand you are a large corporate organization, you will need access to specialist resources on a scale that only a large accountancy firm can provide; and your managers are likely to feel more comfortable dealing with a firm that is, so to speak, in their peer group.

■ But this generalization is far from the whole truth. The fact that a firm is small will not deter large organizations from using its services if it offers valuable expertise in a specialized field. And some corporate clients prefer to obtain their consultancy from seasoned individuals who have acquired a degree of eminence in their professions.

PROFESSIONAL CREDENTIALS: WHAT'S IN A NAME?

Anyone can set himself or herself up as a 'consultant'. How can you tell if a person or a firm is really qualified to give you the help you need?

In the first instance, look at the way they describe themselves. Certain terms such as 'architect' and 'solicitor' have a degree of protection in law and may properly be used for business purposes only by members of the institution that governs a profession.

In the UK the term 'chartered' indicates membership of a professional body that has a royal charter. For example, only Fellows and Members of the Royal Town Planning Institute are allowed to use the term 'Chartered Town Planner'; 'Chartered Accountant' denotes membership of the Institute of Chartered Accountants in England and Wales or of one of its sister institutions in the UK or abroad; and only accountants who are members of the Association of Chartered Certified Accountants (ACCA) may describe themselves as chartered and certified. But the descriptions 'planning consultant' and 'accountant' can be used by any person, whether professionally qualified or not. Readers outside the UK may not be familiar with the term 'turf accountants'. It is seen on the front of betting shops and it's the way bookmakers like to style themselves. Not the people to consult for sound financial advice!

To become a member of a professional institution, a person normally is required to have gained an accredited qualification in the relevant field of expertise – which may demand several years of study and training – as well as a significant amount of practical experience. Many institutions offer different grades of membership, which generally reflect degrees of seniority in the profession. The manner in which a member operates will normally be governed by a code of professional conduct or professional ethics defined by the institution, which will have mechanisms for investigating members accused of misconduct or of performing below necessary levels of competence.

Professional bodies may also place duties and responsibilities on members who are consultants in terms of their relationships with clients – for example, requiring the agreement of written terms of engagement for each contract, a clear statement of the services they are to provide and an explanation of the basis of the fees they charge. Members are usually required to keep up to date with the latest developments in their profession through courses, seminars and training as part of a programme of continuing professional development. In short, using a member of an established professional institution should mean you have an assurance of professional training, performance and conduct.

Most institutions offer a range of services to the public, including client referral services, online directories of member firms and panels in _Yellow Pages_ directories listing registered firms. Your local _Yellow Pages_ directory will have a 'find it fast' section listing professional bodies and trade associations.

Look at the qualifications consultants show on their letterheads and business cards. Do you recognize the letters after a person's name? If not, don't just accept them at face value. Ask the person, or find out for yourself, what they mean and how membership is obtained – what examinations, training and practical experience are required? There is a huge range of fields where either no governing body exists or there is nothing that offers the confidence you would gain from an established institution. Some organizations that call themselves professional bodies have a questionable attitude both to membership and to professionalism: their most demanding entry qualification is often the ability to pay a membership fee. Don't even consider using an adviser whose sole credential is membership of an unknown or untraceable body.

QUALITY ACCREDITATION: WHAT'S IT WORTH?

On letters and brochures from some consultants you may see an ISO 9001 quality mark or an Investors in People logo. What do these mean and are they important?

21

ISO 9001:2000, to use its full reference, is an international standard that sets requirements for quality management and is applicable to all kinds of organizations across all sectors of activity. The ISO 9001 mark tells clients and customers that an organization has in place a quality management system meeting ISO 9001 requirements, and that independent external auditors have assessed its quality management procedures and have certified that these procedures are adhered to throughout its operations. Lloyd's Register Quality Assurance is one of the best-known quality audit and certification companies: there are many other accreditation and regulatory agencies that work in specific fields. An organization may be required to have its quality accreditation reassessed at intervals and to show evidence of continuous professional development.

So far as dealings with clients are concerned, ISO 9001 requires an organization to design and deliver programmes of work that will best fulfil its clients' objectives, to provide clients with adequate information throughout the course of the work, to measure customer satisfaction and to raise levels of customer service. The quality management system has to include detailed statements of the tasks the organization undertakes to perform for the client, in the form of an itemized proposal, as well as a mechanism for logging contacts and communications with the client so as to secure an accurate audit trail.

Investors in People is a UK quality standard that sets a level of good practice for improving an organization's performance through the development of its staff. Achieving this standard, like ISO 9001, is judged on the basis of an external assessment.

The process of gaining quality accreditation demands a substantial investment of time and effort as well as a heavy burden of paperwork, and it can be expensive. Nonetheless even small firms of consultants, including individuals working on their own, have found the investment worthwhile. Because an increasing number of clients now require the firms they use to be quality accredited, this qualification opens the door to consultancy opportunities that would otherwise not be accessible. As a result, quality accreditation has become a potent marketing tool, and for many firms this is its key value.

In theory the discipline of applying method and consistency to the whole of a firm's operations offers benefits in terms of efficiency and productivity. But the fact that a firm has acquired quality accreditation does not necessarily mean that in practice it applies quality management to all that it does. Those who have witnessed a quality assessment from inside a firm may know of instances when an intensive campaign of compliance was engineered in the weeks leading up to and during the assessment, only to have processes return to their usual, less ordered state once accreditation was secured. The individuals working for accredited firms may still be capable of committing basic technical errors, and those errors can often go through the quality management system undetected. So while accreditation does by and large signal a conscientious approach to performance and delivery, the ISO 9001 mark does not in itself indicate that you can take for granted the quality of a firm's technical performance.

There are of course a host of consultants who practise effective quality management and may well fulfil the requirements of ISO 9001, yet have never sought accreditation. Another point to bear in mind, if you are seeking to use consultants in certain scientific and engineering fields, is that not all forms of quality accreditation have the same scope, while there may also be external proficiency qualifications to take into account.

PROFESSIONAL INDEMNITY INSURANCE

Many professional bodies require members in business as consultants to hold professional indemnity insurance, with a sufficient level of cover to ensure that they and their businesses have the means to meet any claim against them – and the means to defend themselves against unsuccessful claims. The Law Society, for example, does not permit solicitors in England and Wales to practise without having professional indemnity insurance in force. Under its current rules, each firm has to secure cover with qualifying insurers to an indemnity limit of £1 million for any one claim. For most firms of consultants, overall liability cover of about £1.5 million will provide enough protection. But the total costs of insurance premiums, when public liability insurance is added to professional indemnity insurance, can represent a significant business expense, particularly for a smaller firm engaged in a relatively low-risk area of professional services.

To protect their interests against any claims that may arise from consultancy work, clients too may require their consultants to hold professional indemnity insurance and may define a minimum level of cover. Though it is better to be overprotected than underinsured, the levels of cover specified by clients are often excessive and out of proportion to the risks likely to be incurred. As a result, small firms that might well be able to offer excellent quality and value for money are discouraged from seeking to work for those clients. Instead of adopting a 'one size fits all' approach, clients would be better served by setting requirements that are more reasonable and more appropriately related to the scale and proposed duration of a contract, the level of risk and the size of a firm.

Depending on their sector of activity, consultants may need to have public liability insurance as well as professional indemnity insurance. When you are considering where to place your work, you will have to judge if there are risks inherent in the work that demand specific forms of insurance cover. Even in today's litigious environment, many fields of consultancy have no history of lawsuits or claims, and it might be a mistake to rule out a consultant – particularly one who is self-employed – simply because he or she does not have liability cover. On the other hand, if there is the smallest possibility that the consultant's work might result in injury, loss of life or damage to property, make sure appropriate insurance cover is in place.

CONSULTANTS AND RELATIONSHIP MANAGEMENT: WHAT YOU NEED TO KNOW

We are used to big supermarket groups harvesting information about our personal tastes and our spending patterns. Consultants have been doing the same for years. It is part of what they call 'relationship management' or 'strategic account management'.

The masters of this art are the big management consultancies. If a client is important enough there will be a relationship team dedicated to capturing and keeping its business. The key principle on which they operate is that every buying decision is ruled essentially by self-interest. Their prime objective is to discover what drives a client manager, what is on his or her personal agenda, what are his or her career priorities – for example, needing to achieve performance targets, wanting to gain a reputation for delivering projects successfully, wanting to climb up the management ladder. Their task then is to convince the manager that these goals can be achieved more effectively by buying services from their firm than by using a competitor.

Their instructions to their staff are on the following lines: 'Your job is to get inside clients' minds. Try to think like them. Work out what motivates them as people. Find out as much as you can about them.

What kind of people are they? What sort of lifestyle do they enjoy? What are their career aspirations? How will their role in the company be strengthened by taking us on as consultants?'

Client relationship teams deploy an armoury of tactics. They use meetings with clients to gauge reactions to their ideas and display their creativity as business advisers. You may be invited to meet them at their offices. These occasions are meant to impress you. A firm will tell its staff to set the stage for the visit and to check that the image given by their offices matches what they are saying to you about the firm's status and achievements. They may be urged to leave copies of technical journals on the table, open at pages highlighting the work of the firm. They may even arrange to have the senior partner appear unannounced at the meeting.

Teams plan programmes of contacts with clients, from regular phone calls to wining and dining at smart restaurants and tickets for sporting and social events. Should people such as secretaries and personal assistants stand in their way and try to prevent them talking directly to you, they work out how they can get past these gatekeepers or bring them round to their side. And when they talk to you, they will do their best to influence how you see your situation so as to lead you to adopt a perspective favouring their particular approach.

Now there is nothing sinister in this, even though some of the methods employed may seem devious. It makes obvious sense for a firm to maintain a dialogue with a potential client so as to learn how it is perceived in terms of performance and value for money, how it can tune its approach to match the client's business priorities and what it can do to improve its quality of service and the value it adds to a business. These are part of the aims of relationship management and they are entirely laudable when expressed openly and honestly.

The problem with the aggressively targeted approach described here is that it can become cynical and manipulative, destroying trust rather than creating it. The consultants' smiles and handshakes may simply conceal their own personal agenda. Any consultant worth his or her salt will want to establish a friendly and constructive relationship with you; and you may be fortunate enough never to encounter relationship management in its more insidious forms. But it is important to be alert to these practices and aware that what may seem an innocent conversation can have an ulterior motive.

What are the skills that consultants find they need most in their day-to-day work?

This was a question posed in a discussion thread on a US-based Web site for professionals working with non-profit organizations. The skill that consultants thought of most value to them was the ability to listen to clients and to use what clients are saying to them to identify the course of action that will work best. One contributor described listening as 'more than just sitting there… it is also shaping questions and pushing the thinking into action… it doesn't matter what the project is, without truly hearing what is going on and being able to interpret it correctly from the beginning, the consultation will be very bumpy'.

Knowing how to manage a client's expectations so that consultants are not asked to meet unrealistic targets and impossible deadlines also ranked high on the list. 'People skills' featured prominently – specifically diplomacy, patience and perseverance, as well as the ability to tell what may be unwelcome truths to people in positions of power. The importance of following through was highlighted by one consultant – 'I always try to deliver a bit more than I promised, a bit earlier than I promised!' Another emphasized the need for consultants to project 'a high level "I'm worth my fee" image', especially if they were at the start of their careers and lacked the confidence that comes with experience.

They might have referred as well to the analytical skills that enable consultants to search out the core elements of a problem and to construct a practical and effective response. There is also a skill that not all consultants possess, which is the ability to foresee what their clients will need and to act quickly and adaptably to meet their requirements.

3

What do consultants charge?

BASIS OF CHARGES: A RANGE OF OPTIONS

When a builder or electrician gives you an estimate for a job, it is normally based on labour charges and the costs of materials. Though materials are rarely a significant item in the charges made by consultants, the costs of labour are as important for them as for other types of businesses. There are a number of ways in which consultants may state the charges for their labour. The two you are likely to encounter most often are fixed prices related to a specific task or package of services, and charges based on the time spent on the work.

Fixed prices

Looked at in simple terms, a fixed price for a consultancy service is like the price of a meal in a restaurant. If you want the chargrilled leg of lamb it will cost you whatever price is shown on the menu. You wouldn't think of asking 'Could we just have £1 worth of the lamb?' or 'If you left out the vegetables, would it cost less?'

Consultants may apply set charges for services that are routine items of activity, where the work is fairly standard, the products of the work clearly defined and the time and resource requirements well understood. In other words, they are offering to do a specific piece of work in a specified time for an agreed price, which may be expressed in terms of a cost limit or budget ceiling. Consultants do not normally volunteer information on how the price is arrived at, just as restaurant owners never tell customers how much the meal costs to make.

The restaurant analogy, though, isn't totally valid. First, the price on a menu is the same for every customer, whatever his or her circumstances, but a consultant may quote different fixed prices to different clients. The price may depend, for example, on whether the client is a private individual or a corporate organization, as well as on the commercial value that the work may have for a particular client. Second, fixed prices may either be all-inclusive, with nothing extra on the bill, or they may relate only to time and labour and not include expenses.

Charging on a fixed price basis is fine if the consultant is confident about the professional effort needed to undertake an assignment, and if the client can be relied on not to make additional or unexpected demands during the course of the work. There is an art in preparing reliable estimates for fixed price work, and it is an art that can be learnt only through error and experience. Consultants carry all or most of the risk if a fixed price contract turns out to demand more resources than they had calculated and overruns its budgeted costs, though they will almost always build a contingency margin into their price to ensure that unexpected problems or changes in the scope of the work do not wipe out their profit on the contract. Clients may prefer charges on a fixed price basis, since it tells them the maximum costs they will incur and helps them limit their exposure to risk, particularly if they are on a tight budget.

The issues that clients need to consider in deciding whether to put work out as a fixed price contract are discussed in Chapter 6.

Time charges

These charges may have an hourly, daily, weekly or monthly basis (Figure 3.1). The longer the work takes, the more it will cost you. It makes sense to avoid an open-ended commitment by asking consultants for an estimate of the time they expect to have to spend on the

Estimated costs of professional time

Position	Name	Estimated input (days)	Day rate (£)	Estimated cost (£)
Team Leader	Johnson	15	650	9,750
Economist	Smith	10	600	6,000
Financial Systems Adviser	Brown	10	650	6,500
Business Development Expert	King	5	800	4,000
Total estimated time costs				**26,250**

Figure 3.1 *Example of time charge basis*

work as well as their rate. Provided they have enough information to give you a reliable estimate, you will then be able to set an agreed budget within which time charges ought to be contained. Be careful, though, not to treat this budget as a form of fixed price. The merit of a time-related basis is its elasticity: if it is found that the work requires significantly more time and effort than was estimated initially, the time charge provides a means of achieving a price that is fair and reasonable both for you and for the consultant. And when a piece of work takes two weeks to complete instead of three, the consultant has an opportunity to demonstrate value and productivity by delivering a cost saving – something that does not happen with fixed price contracts.

Time worked at weekends and unsocial hours is normally charged at the same rate as other hours. Charging an additional sum for 'overtime' would carry the implication that a consultant had been contracted to work for set hours, ie the normal office day, which suggests an employment relationship rather than the status of an independent contractor (Figure 1.2). It is, of course, always open to a consultant to seek to negotiate a specific price for an assignment that is particularly demanding in terms of its deadline: for example, if the consultant is asked late on a Friday to undertake work that has to be delivered on the following Monday morning and will take the whole of the weekend to do. Working intensively to achieve a fast turnaround ought to cost more than delivering work on a routine schedule. If it does not, you may have reason to be concerned about the effort that is being put into the work!

You may find it useful, especially on a long-term assignment, to define the time that a consultant will be expected to spend on your work – say, 20 or 30 hours a week and possibly more if there are urgent targets to be met – but exactly when those hours are worked should be a matter for the consultant to judge.

Both fixed price and time-based contracts may have **award fees** or **incentive fees** built into their terms. Award fees reflect a client's assessment of factors such as service quality, efficiency of delivery, technical enterprise and cost-effective management. Incentive fees reward a consultant for reaching and exceeding targets related to cost control, technical performance and delivery.

Other charge options

These options include various forms of charging based on **percentages**. In sectors of work such as architectural services, the client and consultant may agree a fee that is a percentage of the overall budget for a project, payable in instalments at the completion of each stage in the project. Alternatively, the fee may be related to the commercial value of the work to the client – for example, a percentage of the increase in the development value of a site or property based on an independent valuation. This latter basis is sometimes called a **'value added'** arrangement. Fees may also be calculated on what is termed a **'quantum'** basis, related to a specific schedule of services, outputs and resources.

Clients may sometimes ask consultants to contribute their services to a project for a percentage of its eventual profit or income. This is a risky option for consultants. Apart from the question of what exactly will constitute profit or income, they have learnt to associate this type of arrangement with projects that sadly are unlikely to produce any significant return, and they see themselves as being asked to work on an entirely speculative basis. As a client, you would be well advised to stay clear of this procedure.

Consultants may also work on the basis of an annual or periodic **retainer**, a fee normally paid in advance that entitles a client to call on their services and expertise as and when required.

There are other fields, most notably legal work involving civil court cases and tribunal hearings, where a firm may choose to work on a **'conditional fee'** or 'no win, no fee' basis. In other words, the firm is paid by the client only if the desired result is obtained. In its guidance for clients, the Law Society warns that 'no win, no fee' does not necessarily mean 'no win, no cost': clients who lose their case might have to pay the other side's legal bills and other expenses.

FEE LEVELS

Whichever basis is adopted, the normal level of fees charged by a consultant, whether a firm or an individual, will be influenced by several factors, some of which reflect general considerations applying to all businesses and some of which relate specifically to the characteristics of the client and the work required. The principal factors are:

- the degree of competition inherent in the consultant's professional environment;

- the market value of the expertise on offer, in terms of the demand for the consultant's services;

- the perceived value that the expertise or the work has for the client: for example, where the consultant's expertise may be essential in unlocking the commercial potential of an idea, or where the work is needed to resolve a problem that is so critical that the client cannot afford not to have the work done: in both cases, consultants may feel justified in charging a premium for their services;

- the consultant's business strategy;

- the level of the consultant's operating costs;

- the experience, seniority, professional background and standing of the consultant;

- the nature of the client – for example, whether it is a local community group or a multinational organization;

- the urgency of the work;

- its complexity and degree of technical challenge;

- the duration of the work and the extent to which it offers continuity of income and the scope for cost reductions;

- the degree of commercial risk attached to the work or to the client;

- the location of the work and its impact on overheads.

The interplay of these factors produces a huge range of variation in the fees that are charged by consultants, even for the same services. There is evidence that average charge rates for consultants across a broad range of sectors rose by about 25 per cent over the five years 1998 to 2003. Since the spectrum of services is so broad, attempts to define the extremes of the fee range may seem unhelpful but, in terms of time-based fees, a person in the UK working from home on a routine engagement in a sector of consultancy that is not particularly specialized may find it viable to charge say £200 to £300 a day, whereas the fees that can be obtained for a senior adviser in a field such as corporate banking or reinsurance, where specialist skills are scarce, may be as much as £5,000 or US $8,000 a day. But rates as high as that are rare: in most sectors of consultancy, top-level advice costs considerably less.

Where can you get information about the fees you are likely to incur by using a consultant? In the first instance, by asking individuals or firms directly about their fee levels: what would they normally charge for the work you have in mind, and what is the basis on which their fees are calculated? At the stage of an initial contact you may not be able or prepared to go into detail about the work, and the response may be no more than a rough estimate based on average costs. But it should be enough to tell you how much you may need to budget and where firms stand in terms of relative fee levels.

Secondly, your network of personal and professional contacts may be useful. Do you know people, businesses or other organizations that have engaged consultants for the same type of work? What did they pay and would they recommend the firm they used? These are questions you would in any event want to ask when selecting a consultant (Chapter 5). Lastly, many professional bodies monitor the levels of fees charged by their consultant members, and their consultancy services units may have guidance to offer potential clients.

Check whether a consultant is registered for VAT. If you too are registered and the consultant's services qualify as a business-related purchase, you will be able to reclaim the tax; if you are not registered, the additional cost may influence your willingness to use a consultant who is. Firms normally quote their fees net of VAT. The level of annual turnover at which VAT registration becomes compulsory is usually redefined in each year's Budget statement: at the time of writing (April 2004), the level was £58,000. Firms with total earnings below the threshold level may still choose to register for VAT, so as to be able to reclaim the tax they pay on purchases.

VIEWPOINT

'Quite a few of the inquiries that reach my office concern the fees that consultants charge for their work. People are sometimes unhappy with the bills they receive. In many cases it turns out that they never had a clear agreement with the consultants about exactly what work would be done and what they would be charged. If these matters are left undefined, work can build up and, not surprisingly, fees will escalate. Clients sometimes ask for extra work to be done without being aware of what they will have to pay for it.

'So it is essential to have the scope of the work agreed with the consultants and spelt out in writing, and to get a clear and reliable indication of its cost implications. This is something that many professional bodies require from their consultant members. Clients need to ensure they are happy about the work proposed by consultants before they hire them. They should always be prepared to ask questions about fees, and consultants should always be prepared to give them an honest answer.'

(Consultancy services manager of a professional institution)

HOW FEES ARE CALCULATED

When a firm quotes a rate of say £500 for a day of a consultant's time, how does it work this out? There are normally three elements in the calculation – payroll costs, overheads and profit:

- **Payroll, salary or labour costs** comprise: 1) the gross regular salary plus bonuses paid to the consultant in the office where he or she normally works (or an equivalent target income if the consultant is self-employed); 2) the costs of the non-monetary or fringe benefits paid to staff, which normally include employers' statutory insurance, medical insurance and pension scheme contributions; 3) the costs to the employer of annual leave, sick leave and terminal leave (if taken at the end of an assignment); and 4) vouchers for meals or public transport and other similar items. When a consultant's payroll costs are added up, they often amount to twice his or her basic salary.

- **Overheads** are the business costs not attributable to a specific contract and not reimbursable from a client as distinct cost items. Overheads range from office equipment costs, rent, rates or property taxes and services and utility bills to the costs of professional indemnity and liability insurance, secretarial costs, and the costs of internal management, maintaining quality accreditation, staff training, computer systems, marketing and business development.

- **Profit** is normally calculated as a percentage of the sum of payroll costs and overheads, and is geared to reflect factors such as the degree of exposure to commercial risk inherent in a contract and the value of the work to the client. As a guide, many consulting firms would hope to achieve average profit margins of between 10 and 15 per cent, though the need for keen pricing in a highly competitive market sometimes forces them to accept a more modest return.

The fee calculation simply expresses the fact that the firm needs not just to cover its costs but also to gain a benefit from being in business. The fee level that results from the calculation has to be profitable for the firm, competitive in terms of the market for expertise and reasonable when compared to the funds available to a client. To stay in business for any length of time, a firm cannot afford either to overcharge or to underprice: the aim will be to set a price that reflects quality of performance and expertise, gives an appropriate financial return and matches a client's budget.

There are wide variations in rates between large and small firms as well as regional differences. No two practices are identical in their cost structure or their level of overheads. Large firms tend to have high levels of overheads, reflected in relatively high charge rates.

Where they have a prospect of regular, ongoing work, consultants may be prepared to give a discount on their normal rates. For example, a day rate of £400 may be reduced to £300 if a client can offer, say, 20 or 25 days' continuous work.

The consultant whose diary we glimpsed in Figure 2.2 takes part in his firm's consultancy work both as a technical specialist and as a project manager. The fees that clients are charged for his time are high, partly because they are related to the level of his salary, which reflects his expertise and experience, and partly because the time he commits to non-fee-earning work (for example, business development and management meetings) means that he bears a high burden of overheads.

The relationship between the rate at which an individual is charged out to a client and the costs of the individual's time may be expressed as a **mark-up**. Let us say, for instance, that X is an independent specialist who works as a subcontractor to firm Y. X bills Y £400 for each day that his or her services are supplied to the firm. In turn Y charges its client £550 for each day that X works on a contract. In other words, it applies a mark-up of 37.5 per cent on X's inputs. Mark-ups in the 30 to 50 per cent range are common: in general, the larger the firm, the higher the mark-ups. They represent a contribution toward the firm's overheads and profit and to expenditure such as the costs of bidding for the contract and the costs of quality control and overview by the firm's managers. Most clients prefer to see these high-level, high-cost resources treated as part of overheads rather than billed as chargeable work inputs.

A **multiplier** calculation is another way of expressing the relationship of charge rates to salary costs. The calculation works as follows. Gross salary costs are the basic unit (1.0). Three elements are added to this: 1) social costs and 2) overheads, both expressed as a proportion of gross salary costs (say 0.5 and 1.3 respectively), and 3) profit, expressed as a proportion (say 10 per cent, or 0.28 in this example) of the sum of gross salary costs + social costs + overheads. The multiplier is the sum of the calculation – in this case 3.08. Multipliers are useful in offering clients a means of gauging the degree of consistency in the pricing structure of the bids received from a consultant.

There is a general view among client organizations that the costs of using an external consultant are significantly higher than the costs an organization would incur if a member of its own staff undertook the work. Some clients estimate that the differential can be as much as 200 per cent. What this can buy the client is the added value outlined in Chapter 1 – the expertise, independence and resources that make the business case for using consultants. Moreover, as shown in Chapter 1, the option of doing the work in-house is often neither feasible nor desirable.

HOW TIME IS CHARGED

In consultancy a 'day' normally means either seven, seven and a half or eight hours of chargeable time, depending on one's business arrangements. Consultants often put in rather more than that during the working day, particularly when an output is needed urgently and the deadline is tight. They may charge those hours on an equivalent day basis ('12 hours = 1.5 days') if the client agrees, or they may set a day rate that takes into account the likelihood of working additional hours.

Some consultancy firms require staff working on a day basis to charge either a full day or a half day. For example, if a consultant does two hours' work the client is charged for half a day, and if six or seven hours are worked the charge is for a full day. If you encounter this policy, it is worth questioning the reasoning behind it. Consultants often work on more than one contract at a time; the hours not spent on one client's work can be used for another client; and, if not, those spare hours give the consultant an opportunity to deal with general business matters. Why should you pay for that? On the other hand, many consultants do not count up every last minute they spend on an assignment: if they work an hour or two more than they charge for, that is part of their service to the client.

Time spent on the work is usually interpreted to include, where appropriate:

- time spent on professional work as defined in a contract or letter of engagement (Chapter 6);
- time spent on surveys or data processing;
- meetings with the client and with other firms or persons associated with the work;
- visits to work sites and other relevant locations;
- time spent travelling in connection with the work;
- preparation and production of deliverables, including reports;
- presentations of findings;
- follow-up work as agreed with the client.

So a day charged by a consultant might cover, for example, a two-hour meeting about the work plus four hours spent preparing technical material for the meeting and two hours' travel to and from the meeting.

Most consultants expect to have travelling time paid for at the same rate as other time. It is open to you either to accept that, or to pay a reduced rate (say 50 per cent) of the rate payable for time spent on professional work, or not to pay for travelling time at all. If it is relevant to your work requirements, this is a point that needs to be determined when engaging the consultant (Chapter 6). The mode of travel and the duration of the journey are key criteria. Consultants may argue that time spent travelling is unproductive time that cannot be sold to anyone else. This clearly applies to a short car journey, but three hours on a plane can be spent on chargeable work for another client, on writing a proposal for other work or developing marketing initiatives. Some consultants do not apply time charges for travel within a defined local area.

HOW EXPENSES ARE DEALT WITH

When work is done for a fixed price, the expenses that consultants incur on a job are normally (though not always) covered by the agreed fee and are not billed separately. If the work is done on a time charge basis, expenses are usually repaid by the client either at cost or with the addition of a mark-up, management charge or handling fee. The principle is that consultants meet these expenses out of pocket while they are doing the work, and the client reimburses them when they send in their bill. You may require consultants to identify particular categories of expenses, and may define cost limits for items that are hard to estimate in a reliable way ahead of the start of work.

Remember that we are talking here only about expenses paid out specifically in connection with the work done for you and that are not part of normal overheads. The main types of expenses for which you may have to reimburse consultants include:

- travel and transportation costs such as air or train fares;

- parking charges;

- specific office expenses;

- equipment, materials or supplies purchased, leased or rented specifically in connection with the work;

- the costs of support services bought in from outside, such as laboratory testing, surveys, translation services, legal work and so forth;

- communications, including phone, fax, teleconferencing and data transfer costs;

- computing costs;

- courier services;

- printing and production, including photocopying, scanning and conversion and the presentation of contract-related material in video, CD ROM or other forms;

- documentation, covering the purchase of any necessary documents that you may not be able to supply.

If your work requires a consultant to be away from his or her home or office, you may be asked to pay a daily allowance to cover meals, hotel costs and so forth. This is often termed a subsistence allowance or *per diem*. Consultants have been known to negotiate an agreed *per diem* but then to economize – for example, by staying in budget accommodation – and pocket the balance. You may prefer to tell consultants that you will reimburse subsistence costs only against proof of payment in the form of hotel bills and so forth, and only up to an agreed ceiling.

If air fares are charged separately, it is advisable to require copies of boarding passes before reimbursing them, so as not to find yourself paying business-class fares for individuals who actually flew in economy class. There is also a risk that consultants may charge you the face value of air tickets while obtaining them at a budget price. The best advice is to agree an all-inclusive fee with consultants, rather than paying travel and hotel costs on top of a daily charge. In that way, consultants are free to make their own decisions about how they travel and where they stay, and they avoid any suspicion of overcharging or profiting surreptitiously at your expense.

WILL I HAVE TO PAY MONEY UP FRONT?

In some sectors of consultancy you will be expected to put your hand in your pocket before a start is made on the work. It is a practice one encounters with, for example, some large and specialized legal firms, who may ask for money in advance before they will give any thought to the issues that have brought you to them: their reasons have to do with considerations of risk and their perception of the commercial value of their time. Computer consultants, designers, public relations consultants and advertising agencies too may want an advance payment as a means of securing commitment from clients and as a safeguard in case the fee for the work arrives late. Down payments help to discourage clients who might be regarded as time-wasters and reflect in part the risk that clients may be reluctant to pay for work they either don't like or judge ineffective. An advance payment or upfront deposit of 25 per cent is not uncommon. Normally this money is either held as a security or applied against interim or final invoices.

Consultants may sometimes have to meet significant out-of-pocket expenses before they can start work on an assignment – for example, if it requires them to hire or contract specialized equipment or facilities. In these situations they may look to the client to defray their start-up expenses. They should make this expectation or assumption clear when bidding for the work.

THE HIDDEN COSTS OF CONSULTANCY

Fees and expenses are the principal costs that you face when using a consultant, but they are not the only ones. Drawing up a specification for the work, identifying firms that might meet your requirements, talking to them, assessing their proposals and negotiating a contract – these are all tasks that demand time and resources on your part. They will have costs both in terms of actual expenditure and through the loss of the income you could have gained had you spent the time and resources on your own work.

If you are a business organization, your managers and their staff will have to devote time to administering, monitoring and reporting on the work, as well as holding technical discussions and progress meetings with the consultants. On a large-scale contract, the input of management time will amount to a significant investment.

It may suit you to have consultants work on your premises; you may offer accommodation ranging from individual workstations to an entire office suite; you may put computers, copiers and fax machines at the disposal of the consultants, and provide them with clerical and secretarial assistance. These too represent costs that are easily lost sight of, but they all need to be taken into account when assessing the value for money of a consultancy assignment.

Whenever you engage a consultant, you will incur to a greater or lesser extent costs that are additional to the sums of money shown on invoices. This is inescapable and it should not discourage you from using consultancy services. Be aware of these costs and try to make sure that time and resources are used as productively as possible to secure the results you intend.

COUNTING THE BENEFITS

Because the benefits gained by using consultants can be so much harder to express in monetary terms than their costs, it is understandable that clients may view their engagement as an item of expenditure rather than a business investment. But the return that clients obtain from the services of consultants can repay many times over the fees that are paid. Taking their advice can help you save money and generate new revenue by focusing your efforts on better ways of doing things, on more efficient modes of operation and on more productive systems and technologies.

Case Study

After leaving the advertising agency that had employed him for several years, Martin S set up in business as a self-employed graphic designer, working from home in a network with other professionals. A colleague at work recommended to him a firm of accountants that specialized in tax planning for small businesses. Martin visited their office to see if they could give him guidance on his tax affairs and accounts as well as help him prepare a business plan. He met one of the partners and asked the firm to act as his accountants.

For some time he was happy with the relationship: his accountants seemed to be giving him useful advice, they dealt promptly with his tax affairs and their fees were within his means. When the accountancy firm moved to a new office near Canary Wharf in London's Docklands, Martin noticed that their fixed charges increased, but since his own business was at the time relatively buoyant he accepted the situation. Then his work flow suffered a downturn; with less money coming in, he found it difficult to meet their fees as easily as in the past; he began to send them small amounts on account, and needed frequent reminders from them about clearing the outstanding balance.

A year or two ago the accountancy firm was absorbed into a financial services group, which assured clients that the firm would now be able to offer them access to a far wider range of investment management, financial advice and accountancy services. But as Martin had expected, the change brought a further sizeable rise in their fees and, instead of the office accountant phoning sympathetically about his overdue payments, he was now receiving impatient letters from the 'group credit controller'.

He knew it really was not fair to keep them waiting, and he did send them money whenever he could, but at heart he resented the mounting costs of their services and the fact that the fixed fee basis on which they charged was largely unexplained. They could hardly have been unaware of his financial position, since they were responsible for preparing his business accounts! Moreover, they now seemed less attentive to him as a client, which he attributed to having been branded a bad payer. Whereas formerly he had dealt directly with the partner, the people now drawing up his accounts and tax returns were relatively junior. If that was because preparing his accounts was a simple and straightforward job, he wondered, why did it have to cost so much? What had been a small firm focusing on services to other small businesses appeared to have changed its character and to be no longer interested in him.

When his business friends told him how cost-effective their accountants were, Martin could only try to rationalize the situation by reminding himself that as a creative professional he had always found financial matters foreign to his nature, that his accountants at least appeared to have a good relationship with the Revenue, and that moving away from them would probably be a messy and complicated process.

He now has a local accountant who seems no less competent and charges fees that he finds more manageable. He regrets that he didn't make the move earlier. His advice to anyone in the same position is not to feel inhibited or embarrassed about questioning the level of fees or inquiring about the basis on which they are calculated. He acknowledges that he was largely responsible for the deterioration in the relationship with his former accountants, and thinks the problem might have been avoided had he approached them directly to see if they might be able to offer an 'economy' service matched to his budget.

4

How should I specify the job to be done?

Before you approach a consultant, or even decide whom to approach, you need to have a fairly clear idea of the work you want to have done, when you want it done, the results you want it to achieve and the money that is available to pay for it. In short you need first to think the work through. This means thinking about the details – not just the broad picture – and recognizing that small jobs can demand as much analysis and preparation as large ones.

Deciding your requirements may be a straightforward matter, and putting them in words may take only a sentence or two. But you still need to make sure your intentions and expectations are expressed clearly enough to leave no room for doubt or misunderstanding. If the work is likely to be complicated, stating your requirements may mean producing a document that itemizes them point by point, and this may run to several pages. In this book this type of document – whether short or long – is called a 'work specification': it is what many clients and consultants call a 'brief' or 'terms of reference'.

PREPARING A WORK SPECIFICATION

The work specification has a precise function, which is to focus your view of your requirements so that you can communicate them accurately to the person or people who will be doing the work. It offers two key benefits. First, it helps you think out your priorities: when you face consultants to talk about the work, they will see that you have a clear idea of what is important to you. Second, it helps limit the risk of getting results that fail to match your objectives: in its absence, the outcome of a contract may be what consultants think you need rather than what you actually want. Figure 4.1 shows the relationship of the work specification to other elements in the consultancy process.

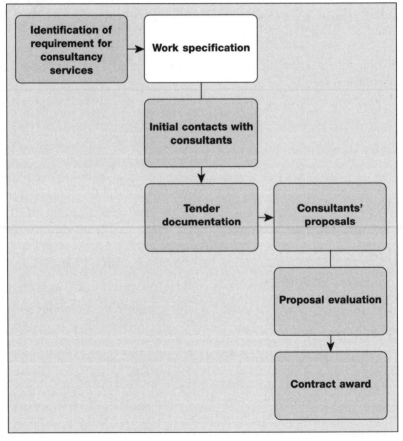

Figure 4.1 *Relationship of the work specification to other elements in the consultancy process*

A good consultant will generally produce good work despite being given a poor work specification – and conversely, a good work specification alone will not be sufficient to defend you from the damage that an ineffective consultant can do. But it is obviously in your interests to try to get the specification right and to do so at the very start, rather than setting out with some indeterminate notion and hoping your requirements will become clearer once the work takes shape. When a work specification is direct and businesslike, it sends signals about your good sense and seriousness as a client. The sharper the focus on your requirements, the greater the prospects of success.

Don't make the mistake of using identical work specifications every time you plan a particular type of assignment. There may be a close resemblance between one job and another; the technical requirements may be similar; and previous specifications may offer a useful model to adapt. But in every case there will be points to consider that are particular to that individual piece of work, and these need to be reflected in the content of the work specification. By all means, consult previous specifications if you have some to hand, but treat them just as a platform for ideas.

Producing an effective work specification involves a sequence of tasks:

- defining the objectives of the work;

- drawing up its scope and content;

- gauging the practical demands of the work;

- setting a timetable for the work;

- identifying the right form of engagement;

- confirming your budget;

- determining what you will need to do to help the work succeed;

- deciding your critical requirements;

- assessing the risks that might interfere with your plans;

- taking measures to reduce the risks;

- putting the work specification on paper.

This chapter reviews each of these tasks in turn.

DEFINING YOUR OBJECTIVES

What do you want to get out of the work? What do you see as its outcome? Express your needs and objectives in terms of the results, changes and benefits the work is intended to produce, not in terms of the services a consultant can provide. Keep your objectives firmly in mind while developing the work specification. When there are options to examine and choices to make, ask 'Which is most likely to achieve the results we want?'

Be open and honest about your motives. If you try to obscure them, you have more to lose than to gain: you will devalue the work specification, and you may appear to be a client who is muddle-headed or, even worse, devious.

Don't let stray and possibly spurious aims attach themselves to the work ('If we're bringing in designers to produce our report and accounts, why don't we get them to look at our public relations at the same time?'). They are likely to blur the focus of your intentions.

DRAWING UP THE SCOPE AND CONTENT

In many and perhaps most instances we will not be aware of the detailed tasks and activities that go into the work. We know we require a service and an end-product – our business accounts prepared, a planning appeal lodged or a will drafted, for example – but we probably don't have a clear understanding of the individual tasks that a consultant or adviser has to undertake in delivering the product. This is particularly the case when the work involves processes of analysis that are open to the use of different methods and techniques, each of which may yield different results. So we are unlikely to be in a position to say *how* we want each task performed. But we do need to make clear exactly *what* we want done, and we then have to trust that the consultant will go about things conscientiously and efficiently.

There are other situations in which the work may be within our own competence so that we have a good knowledge of the process needed to deliver it. This is likely to be the case, for instance, when the use of external consultants is motivated by constraints on our time or resources or by the need for independent judgement. We may then want to make certain that the work follows the most direct, practical and cost-effective route to its intended results; but in defining our

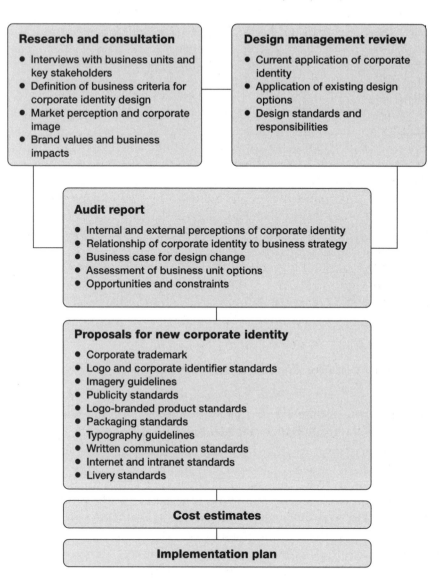

Figure 4.2 *Example of a basic work structure*

requirements it is important not to express them in terms so broad that they invite misinterpretation or so narrow that they are rigidly prescriptive.

If there is any degree of complexity about an assignment, divide the work into its main structural parts so as to create manageable packages of work or groups of tasks (Figure 4.2). Each work package needs to have clear objectives and produce at least one well-defined output. You might treat as an initial contract the piece of work that gets the process started (eg the audit and review in Figure 4.2) so as to be able to judge the effectiveness of a consultant without becoming involved in a substantial commitment.

Project management software can help you trace the critical path through the work and allow you to explore the outcomes of different options and priorities by asking 'What if?' or 'Where do we go from here?' and testing the results.

The questions to ask yourself at this stage are:

- What are the options or alternatives for structuring the work? There may be several possible approaches or solutions. What information will you need to be able to identify the one likely to be the most practical and cost-effective?

- What are the resource implications of these options?

- Which tasks will form the core of the work, in terms of the professional effort required?

- Which tasks are likely to be the most critical to the success of the work?

- Can the work be fast-tracked – are there parts of it that can be undertaken simultaneously to achieve early results?

- Are there external constraints on the way the work will have to be performed – for example, legal, security, environmental or health and safety requirements?

- What risks are associated with the work, and which are the tasks most likely to expose it to risk?

While the work will suffer if you leave this analysis until the last minute, you need to be sure that you have a sound enough fund of information to make the analysis reliably, and that the situation is not likely to change significantly by the time the work is due to start. Specifications that are developed prematurely will not prove a viable basis for undertaking the work.

GAUGING THE PRACTICAL DEMANDS OF THE WORK

Consultants are sometimes heard to complain that clients have no idea of the amount of effort a task entails, and as a result expect an unsustainable pace of work and unrealistically fast delivery times at an unreasonably low cost. To ensure that your view of the work is sensible and practical, consider the following points:

■ Do you have the measure of the resources needed to do the work and manage its delivery efficiently? Can it be undertaken by a single person or will it call for a team of consultants?

■ If a team effort will be needed, how should the team be structured?

■ What skills, knowledge, attitudes and experience will be required on the part of the consultants performing the work and the people on your side managing and administering it?

■ Have you or your business colleagues commissioned similar work before? Are there aspects of the work that have caused problems in the past?

■ How will you know if the consultants are doing a competent job and if the work is achieving the results you intend?

■ What assumptions are you making about the information to hand or the conditions in which the work will have to be done? Are you sure you know the facts of the present situation well enough to identify the extent of whatever changes the work will produce? Are the data on which you are relying up to date and valid? Or will the delivery programme need to include tasks that provide this information and define a baseline for the work?

■ Where will the work be done? Will new office space and equipment be needed?

■ Are there, for whatever reason, seasonal factors or other time considerations that need to be taken into account?

Make a careful assessment of the items or services that you will want the consultants to produce. 'Deliverables', as they are termed, can be products such as reports and other documents, or services such as training programmes, management seminars, laboratory testing, contract management and so forth.

What deliverables will you need in order to obtain the answers you require, to provide a confident basis for decisions on the part of your organization, and to enable the results of the work to be communicated effectively? Structure these deliverables into a schedule that matches your requirements for information at key decision-points and that will enable you to audit the technical basis of the work and the effectiveness of the consultants' management procedures. Thinking these issues through before the work starts can save you having to vary the terms of a contract later on.

SETTING A TIMETABLE

If you have enough information, try to estimate how much time should be needed to undertake the work. You will not want the work to take any longer than it has to, but you also need to remember that a fast turnaround may not always give you the best result in terms of quality or practicality. People or firms in your contact network may be able to help you on this point. Later you will want to use this time estimate in assessing the work schedule that a consultant may outline. If you have calculated that a job should take one person a week to do, and a consultant proposes to use five people on it for a month, either one or other of you has badly misjudged your requirements or the consultant is attempting to inflate the job at your expense.

Decide how quickly you need results. If the work is intended to help you meet a deadline, that deadline will set the latest acceptable completion date. You will need to have a good solution within that time; the option of waiting longer for the best solution to emerge will not be feasible. From your assessment of the scale of the work, you should be able to calculate the time its performance is likely to take, and so arrive at the date by which work will need to have started. If this starting date looks practicable, you can draw up a timetable for the work. Mark on the timetable any clearly defined stages in the structure of the work and the target dates when the results of each stage have to be delivered. Build in contingency margins to allow for possible delays. You also need to make sure that there are points along the route of the work where you can, if necessary, tell the consultant 'Stop, we've gone far enough with you' (Chapter 7).

When thinking about the starting date, remember that a consultant – particularly one whose services are much in demand – may well have a full order book and is unlikely to be sitting by the phone waiting for clients to call. Unless the situation is urgent, you may have to be patient until the people who are right for the job are able to roll up their sleeves and start on your assignment, though in the meantime they may be able to talk to you about the work.

Thinking ahead to the contract or letter of engagement, identify the action that will formally mark the start of the work and the output that will mark its completion. If it is a large-scale assignment requiring the services of a team, they may need a period in which to get mobilized and ready for the start of work.

IDENTIFYING THE RIGHT FORM OF ENGAGEMENT

Most requirements can be met by a clearly defined engagement to undertake a specific piece of work. There are two other forms of engagement that may be appropriate in circumstances where there is likely to be a continual or at least recurring need for professional assistance. The first is to set up a 'call-off' contract, in other words engaging a consultant to provide services at your request as and when required and generally over a fixed term. This means you will have in place a mechanism that can respond quickly to an unexpected need for assistance as well as dealing with scheduled tasks. Call-off contracts are discussed in Chapter 6. The second form of engagement is to secure professional services through a retainer (Chapter 3), for which a consultant agrees either to spend no less than a defined amount of time on your work (for example, six days a month) or to be available to you as and when required.

CONFIRMING YOUR BUDGET

Purchasing consultancy and professional advice is like any other transaction. You need to weigh the likely expense of the work against the funds at your disposal and then decide the most cost-effective course of action.

Do your best to get a reliable indication of what the work should cost. Perhaps you have recently engaged a consultant for similar work and so have a good idea of going rates. Other people or organizations that have had work done may be able to give you information. Use your network of personal and professional contacts to help develop cost estimates.

Obtaining dependable advice on costs is particularly critical if the work involves tasks and activities with which you are unfamiliar. You may have to invest an appreciable amount of time to reach the right answer; but it is an investment that may well save you money later. Whether the eventual contract for the work is based on a fixed price or on time charges, the assignment is unlikely to yield its intended results if you have significantly underestimated the costs of performing the work satisfactorily.

How you use cost information will depend on the significance that costs have in your buying decision. Is the work task-driven ('It has to be done, and we just have to find the money')? Or is it budget-driven ('We have no more than x pounds or dollars available for the work, and it must be held within that limit')? Do you try to add to the money you have available – for example, by dipping into savings or cash reserves, increasing an overdraft limit or securing a higher budget allocation – or do you decide you are planning beyond your means and trim down your requirements?

Whatever your decision, you need to make sure that the tasks set out in the work specification match the funds you have available, and that you get the best value from every penny you invest in the work.

Bear in mind also the costs of producing the items that you may want consultants to deliver. For example, if high-quality reports and presentations are important, you should obtain up-to-date information about the current rates for reprographics, media production, design support, image setting and so forth. Include an appropriate sum in your budget estimate so that you have an accurate basis on which to judge the cost figures put forward by consultants.

If it is to be realistic, an overall estimate of costs has to take account of the likelihood that your initial ideas about the work will change as your plans take shape. The work may involve tasks that you have not expected as well as items that have an uncertain scope and carry significant levels of risk. For these reasons, you would be well advised to add a contingency of, say, 10 or 15 per cent in arriving at your total budget.

When you are evaluating competitive bids and comparing prices (Chapter 5), keep this budget figure in mind as a form of yardstick. Provided your estimates are sound, it will generally be close to a reasonable 'should pay' price.

DETERMINING YOUR INPUTS

It is not only the consultants who need to put time and resources into the work. There is always a contribution that the client has to make, as noted in the observations on hidden costs in Chapter 3. Even a simple job will require a management effort on your part to set the work up and see it through. A large-scale or complex assignment may call for logistical support both to help get the work off the ground and to ensure that consultants have ready access to contacts, information and facilities.

Depending on the nature of the assignment, logistical support may need to include:

- administrative and secretarial assistance: you will have to think about the best way of managing this support, how many staff you will provide and to whom they will report;

- data processing services: matters such as access to computer systems will need to be thought through carefully before the work starts;

- access to offices, staff, documentation, communication networks, Internet services and in-house technical assistance;

- copying, scanning and document production services – for example, through an in-house reprographics unit;

- laboratory and testing facilities.

Having consultants on your own premises can offer benefits in terms of logistics and the development of working relationships, particularly if your personnel and the consultants are part of a joint team. You will have direct access to people, ideas and feedback, and you should find it easier to monitor the approach the consultants are taking and to assess how well the work is being performed. One drawback of this arrangement is that consultants may, simply by virtue of their presence, learn information about your business or about matters related or unrelated to the work that may put you at a disadvantage in managing it.

Data and documentation represent a key category of input. When bidding for the work, consultants will expect to receive an accurate picture of your requirements and their context so that they can prepare an efficient competitive response. When they have won the contract, they will need copies of records, plans, reports and other material related to the job in hand in order to make a purposeful start on the work.

DECIDING WHAT IS REALLY IMPORTANT

If it is essential that the work is done in a particular way – for example, to meet legal obligations, quality standards, environmental constraints or health and safety factors – this is a point you will need to specify firmly and precisely. There may be performance criteria on which you are not prepared to compromise, or the completion date may be a matter that allows no scope for negotiation. Identify the critical success factors – the points likely to have a critical bearing on the outcome of the work or likely to expose you to unacceptable risk. Make sure the work specification spells these points out in a way that leaves no doubt about your demands.

You will normally want to specify the outputs of the work – the results to be achieved – and the items or services that are to be delivered by the completion date. But there are areas of work such as research and development where the results that are sought are novel approaches and fresh ideas. It may not be practicable or desirable to define the outputs of the work to any specific level of detail, in case you defeat the purpose of the assignment by limiting the scope for creativity and innovation.

In most contexts, the work specification will need to offer a degree of flexibility, so as to enable the work to benefit from new ideas and adapt to changes in the requirements of the situation. If you take on good consultants, they will expect you to know what you want to achieve, but not necessarily how to achieve it: this is where their expertise comes in, guiding you along the most direct and cost-effective route to the intended results. They may, for example, be able to indicate ways in which you can obtain results more quickly or more economically and no less dependably than your own timetable or estimates of staffing might suggest. When you apply work specifications in trying to select the best people to do the job, you need to look for convincing evidence of professionalism and a sound basis for trust. The better you know the people who are to do the work, and the greater your confidence in their professional quality, the less reason you will have to want to specify the work in every last detail.

With any type of assignment, there will be items that no one is able to determine at the initial stage of preparing the work specification. Factors outside your control may force second thoughts or shifts in the scope or direction of the work. A need may emerge for specialist expertise in additional fields. Information may come to light that requires a fresh approach to parts of the work. These and other reasons underline the need for clients to keep the work specification under review throughout the assignment.

ASSESSING AND CONTROLLING RISKS

Risk can be defined as the possibility that something unwelcome will occur to impair or disrupt the achievement of your objectives. The term covers various types of damage, not just financial loss. If you can identify the risks inherent in an assignment and assess their likely impact on the work and on your business, you can then develop measures that may enable you to manage and reduce them.

Certain risks will be resistant to control, and in some instances the measures needed to manage them may be uneconomic. You will then have to decide whether to accept them or rethink the scope of the work. But it is possible to protect yourself from other risks by thinking ahead, asking what could go wrong and planning to forestall problems.

Your experience of similar work may point to items that caused difficulties in the past or are hard to get right or manage effectively. The fault may lie as much within your own organization and its attitude to getting jobs done as with the people who undertake the work. The question to address is how you can write safeguards into the work specification so as to minimize these risks or at least reduce them to an acceptable level. Taking preventative action in this way is part of the process of risk management, and it is one of the keys to best practice in work specification. The more thought that is given at the start to reducing risk, the less the need later on for damage limitation and fire-fighting.

When you reach the stage of drawing up a contract, you may want consultants to accept either full or partial responsibility for risks that you believe are critical and that can be managed more effectively by them than by you (Chapter 6). Most contracts involve a balance of risk ownership between the two parties, even contracts in which financial risk is assigned to the consultants. Large-scale contracts may require the preparation of a detailed risk management plan as well as risk ownership tables showing how risks are to be allocated.

The following are the most common risks that you should try to control.

Work overrunning the time scheduled for completion

- Consultants may be late in starting or slow in progressing the work.

- Technical difficulties may hold up its completion: the work may turn out to be harder to perform than either you or the consultants had realized.

- Inputs that are due to be provided by you or the consultants may arrive late.

- Outputs may not be delivered on time.

Manage these risks by:

- Making the required start and completion dates explicit in the work specification and in the eventual contract.

- Setting targets and milestones that are realistic and achievable.

- Ensuring you are aware as early as possible of technical problems, particularly if they are likely to affect critical deadlines, so that you and the consultants can try to put into place the necessary resources and skills to get back on course (Chapter 7).

- Stressing the need for the right people and other resources to be available at the right time.

- Ensuring that the consultants receive on schedule whatever inputs are due to come from you – whether they are documents, office facilities, staff time or administrative services.

Costs overrunning your budget

- Costs may escalate beyond the agreed price.

- The budget may be spent at a rate that does not match the progress of the work.

Manage these risks by:

- Making the consultants bear the risk of cost escalation. This will normally be the case when the work is to be undertaken for a fixed price, though a long-term assignment may allow periodic price reviews.

- Requiring accurate monitoring and reporting of the rate at which your budget is being spent.

- Underlining the need for openness and transparency in time-keeping, records and accounts.

Resource deficiencies

- The people who do the work may turn out to be inadequate in respect of their number, capabilities, experience or attitude. They may seem to be learning their job at your expense, expecting you to do their thinking for them or merely analysing information at a superficial level instead of bringing an informed perspective to the work.

- They may be poor at communicating their results.

- They may be subject to competing work demands and not put their best effort into the job. Individuals may not be able to provide their inputs as scheduled, or may depart to other work or other forms of employment before their role in the assignment is completed.

- Some of the work may be fed to subcontractors, who may prove variable in terms of output, quality, motivation or availability.

- The work programme may suffer delay and disruption if sub-contractors are paid late or erratically.

Manage these risks by:

- Emphasizing in the work specification and the contract that payment in full will depend on quality performance and efficient delivery.

- Where appropriate, requiring the consultants to provide evidence that the people who are put forward are competent to do the work efficiently and to the standards that you set. This may mean that their bids and proposals have to include detailed CVs, certified as correct, as well as letters of commitment that the individuals named in a team will be available to fulfil their inputs as indicated in the work plan.

- Specifying that the consultants will be expected to have in reserve personnel of equivalent competence who can be assigned to the work should an individual fall ill or meet with an accident.

- Requiring individuals to be fully conversant with whatever software, equipment or specialist techniques they may need to use for the performance of their work.

- Requiring the consultants to identify any firms or individuals to whom they propose to subcontract part of the work. The requirement is sometimes related to the value of the subcontracted work – for example, where it is likely to amount to more than 20 or 25 per cent of the total fee. But this value is often hard to estimate reliably, and there remains a risk that unidentified subcontractors may be entrusted with services that represent only a small proportion of the total fee but are highly critical in terms of their impact on the success or failure of the work. It is preferable to require across-the-board naming of proposed subcontractors.

- Requiring information about the proposed subcontractors' other clients – there may be conflicts of interest.

- Stipulating that, where subcontractors are involved, you expect to see back-to-back contracts, ie the consultants will be accountable for the performance of subcontractors just as if they were their own staff.

- Including in the contract a requirement for the consultants to pay subcontractors regularly and promptly.

Ineffective working relationships

- There may be aspects of the work where responsibilities overlap, are ill defined or fall into gaps between the roles of individuals.

- Tension may develop between your staff and the consultants.

- Failures in communication may cause misunderstanding and a lack of trust.

- The consultants may not fully grasp what you want to achieve.

- Resources may be wasted through an inefficient approach to the work.

Manage these risks by:

- Maintaining clear lines of communication, a transparent process of dialogue and direct channels of accountability.

- Arranging progress meetings (Chapter 7): on large-scale assignments, you may find it useful to set up regular forums where work issues can be discussed in an open but formal manner.

- Making it clear in the work specification and the contract who will be responsible for managing what.

- Checking that no task is left unmanaged.

- Explaining the purpose of the work to people in your organization (Chapter 1).

- Writing the work specification and the contract in a way that removes any room for interpretation about the benefits the work is intended to produce, how it is to be performed and your relationship with the people who will undertake it.

- If the assignment is long term, requiring an early inception report setting out a definitive programme for achieving the work (Chapter 7).

- Making sure the course of the work can be adjusted and redirected, if necessary, in response to changes in its environment.

Inadequate outputs

■ Consultants may not deliver the right outputs to meet your requirements.

■ Performance may fall below the expected quality.

■ Technical methods and findings may be questionable or may conflict with work done by other consultants.

Manage these risks by:

■ Stating clearly the outputs and deliverables that you require.

■ Structuring the work into performance-related packages: for example, specifying that if the consultants do not deliver competent results in Stage 1 they will not be considered for further stages.

■ Measuring output and comparing performance to what was agreed in the contract.

■ Asking the consultants to prepare a quality plan for the delivery of the work.

■ Requiring an appropriately detailed technical justification for the consultants' findings and recommendations.

These are all points that can and should be made explicit in the work specification and in an eventual contract for the work (Chapter 6).

PUTTING THE WORK SPECIFICATION ON PAPER

The process outlined thus far should have resulted in a preliminary version of your work specification. This will help you decide whom to approach about the work and it will form the basis of the information that you will need to give consultants if you invite them to quote or tender for the work (Chapter 5). But you first need to feel confident that you have gauged your requirements sensibly. It will do no one any good if you discover late in the day that the specification was inadequate.

Check that you haven't missed out any important points, but don't worry at this stage about getting every detail right. When you are selecting consultants you will have an opportunity to discuss your requirements with them and explore how they might address the work. They can then help you gain a more focused view of what needs to be done to meet your objectives.

There may sometimes be advantages in enlisting outside help with the development of a work specification, for example by engaging consultants to assist your staff or to prepare material on particular aspects of the work. These advantages will be evident where a specification has to be drawn up for a type of assignment or field of activity with which your organization is unfamiliar. Consultants may identify issues about procedures and timescales that you had not taken into account and may be able to suggest approaches that can save you time and money, particularly where different methods and techniques have different implications in terms of their costs and usefulness.

Bringing in consultants for this purpose can be recommended in situations where you know them well and have confidence in their professionalism; where there is no possibility of a conflict of interest; and where they understand clearly your intentions and expectations. In other words, a relationship of trust needs to have been established for this course of action to produce a successful outcome. The fact that consultants have had a hand in the work specification will usually be apparent to those bidding for the work. If you do use consultants for the work specification, make sure that you or a member of your in-house staff understands the work well enough to answer directly any questions you may be asked by bidders so that you don't have to refer back continually to your source of advice.

There are now two questions to be decided: 1) Who will manage the drafting of the specification? 2) Who is to be responsible for writing, editing and coordinating the draft? These will often, though not always, be the same person. If the work is straightforward, it should be feasible for one person to manage and produce the work specification single-handed. But if you are dealing with a large-scale or complex project, framing its specification will almost certainly involve a team effort that may have to draw on a range of skills. Depending on the specific circumstances of the work and the character of the organization, the responsibility for developing the work specification may fall on the manager commissioning the work, on a technical expert in a key business field or on someone skilled in drafting and producing this type of document. If you have one person who combines these attributes, so much the better.

In a corporate organization the way the work specification is phrased may need the approval or endorsement of other managers and decision

Scope of the work	• What you want done • Why you want it done • What results and benefits you want from the work • What its basic components are • What questions have to be answered • Information on background and context • Facts and figures • Tasks and activities • Interest and challenges of the work
Approach and method	• Who will be responsible for what • What skills and competencies you want applied • Any requirements for specific procedures • Emphasis on quality management and efficient delivery • Record keeping • Progress monitoring and review • *Requirement to name subcontractors* • *Compliance with standards*
Timetable	• When you want the work done • Start and completion dates • Targets and milestones
Deliverables	• What the consultants have to produce
Inputs	• What you will provide – eg data, assistance, access to services

Figure 4.3 *Basic structure of a work specification*

makers. To make your life easier, think about the forms of wording they would expect to see in the document or that echo corporate philosophy. If the work is to be funded by some other unit within your business, it is essential that the required outcome, as defined in the work specification, coincides with what they believe they are paying for.

Structuring and writing the work specification is a matter of observing five basic principles:

- **Clarity.** As emphasized at the start of this chapter, set out your requirements clearly and in a way that permits only one interpretation – the precise meaning that you intend.

- **Balance.** Make sure each aspect of the work receives due emphasis, and that the level of detail is in proportion to the significance of the topic. Remember that the work specification is meant to be _used_, rather than existing just as part of an administrative process, and that the people who use it will be searching for signals about what you consider important.

- **Logical progression.** Present information in a sequence that is businesslike, ordered and consistent.

- **Comprehensiveness.** Check that you have included all the points needed to make the work specification an efficient technical document, but keep out surplus detail. This can be defined as information that does not assist the performance or achievement of your requirements.

- **Conciseness and brevity.** Where the work specification is intended for a knowledgeable consultant with whom you have a good professional relationship, it may consist of only a page or two, even for a large-scale assignment. Where it will go out to a number of other consultants, you may have to explain more and write more.

Whether the work specification is a single page or a sizeable document, it has to provide enough information to allow consultants to make an effective competitive response. Figure 4.3 outlines a basic structure that should serve for work specifications in most contexts.

First, you need to explain the **scope of the work**. Describe what you want done, why you believe it is necessary, and what outcome you expect from the work. The starting point for this description is the analysis that you made earlier when thinking the work through and determining its structure. If the work has successive stages, describe each stage in turn.

Try to inject a sense of interest into the way you describe the work. Draw attention to any challenges that are part of it – not in a negative manner, but in a way that points to the professional value of undertaking the assignment.

63

Give some of the history behind your requirements, so that the people using the work specification can understand how things have developed and why, what work has been done so far and what remains to be done. Provide supporting facts and figures.

As part of a risk management strategy, indicate any requirements you may have in terms of the consultants' **approach and method** – the way the work or a task is to be performed. But take care to limit this to items that have to be specified and cannot be left to the consultants' judgement, as discussed above. Remember that your job is to explain what work you need from the consultants rather than to instruct them about methodology. Don't prescribe more than you absolutely need to, and don't try to impress them with your knowledge of their specialization.

Points that might be covered in this part of the work specification include:

- the consultant's professional or technical responsibilities and the extent of your responsibilities as client;

- the level of professional resources that you would expect to be applied to the work – for example, the size and structure of the consultant team;

- the skills and competencies needed by the consultants;

- whether you require a particular procedure or method to be adopted in undertaking the task;

- items on which you may be seeking an innovative approach;

- quality management measures to secure the efficient delivery of results;

- arrangements for record keeping, progress monitoring and review;

- whether you require the consultants to name subcontractors they might propose to use;

- whether people are required to work to particular international or national standards, operating principles or defined safety procedures.

If the consultancy work needs to be undertaken by a team, it is particularly important to define the competencies and qualities you expect from the person leading the team, since his or her personality and management skills can have a decisive impact on its performance.

These competencies should include proven management ability, interpersonal and communication skills, adaptability and the capacity to cope with pressure, as well as technical authority gained through successful experience of team leadership on recent assignments.

Indicate your required **timetable** for the work or services, based on a realistic assessment of the time and level of professional effort needed to achieve a satisfactory result. Consider whether you want to encourage consultants to offer completion in a shorter time span.

State your required start and completion dates, if appropriate. The start may be expressed either as a calendar date or in terms such as 'not more than x days after the receipt of instructions to proceed' or 'immediately upon award of contract'. The completion date may be the date when the final deliverable of the work is to be supplied or the date when the assignment is considered to be operationally closed. If the work programme is a sequence of stages, indicate their target completion dates and deadlines as well as the time you may require for review and approval.

Make it clear what you will expect in the form of **deliverables**. Ensure that the technical and management aspects of the work are covered adequately, but keep the requirements for deliverables in proportion to the time and resources available. The effort needed to produce a continuous stream of management reports might be better devoted to the work itself.

When writing about the work as a whole – for example, in introducing the work specification – you may wish to refer to it as a **minimum specification**, using words such as 'The tasks to be undertaken by the consultant shall include but not be limited to. . .' or 'The scope of work describes the client's minimum requirements. . .'. This approach recognizes that your requirements may evolve as the work takes shape, and that, as noted earlier in the chapter, not all the tasks needed to make the assignment succeed may be evident at the time of preparing the work specification. It should also encourage consultants, when developing their proposals, to consider what they can deliver over and above the minimum specification as a means of adding value to their services.

If there are items or issues that you particularly wish not to be addressed by the consultants, make it clear that they are excluded from the work specification.

MOVING AHEAD TO SELECTION

The next step is to decide how you want to take forward the process of choosing your consultants. Will you have to research the field or do you already know people qualified to do the work? Who will undertake this task – you or someone else in your organization? Will an interview or an exchange of e-mails or letters be enough, or will you require a formal written proposal? What will govern your choice – value for money, timing, cost or a combination of factors? These questions are followed up in the next chapter.

Case Study

The client was an independent record company that intended to set up an interactive Web site where visitors could search its catalogue, listen to tracks from new and recent releases, download audio files and read interviews with artists and news about the company. An in-house team had been set up to plan and implement the project, but after a year they had made scant progress and had little to show except notes of meetings with Internet consultants and initial ideas about developing an Internet marketing strategy and designing the site.

The managing director called in management consultants to review the team's work and determine what needed to be done to develop the site and bring it into operation. The work specification they were given was brief – just one paragraph! – and to the point: 'What are the technical options? Should we manage the site ourselves or use an external service? Which option will serve the company best? What are the cost implications? How soon can we have a professionally designed site up and running? What steps do we need to take to implement it?' He asked the consultants to give him answers within a month.

Following a rapid and intensive programme of research, analysis and evaluation, the consultants identified a preferred option, drew up a table of cost data, outlined an implementation plan and sent in their report exactly four weeks after starting work. The MD's initial reaction was silence. Then an e-mail came in from his office: 'Why haven't you given me what I asked for? I wanted all the options costed, and I need that information in a comparative table showing bottom-line figures for all cost elements of each option.'

The consultants looked again at the wording of the work specification. That innocent-sounding phrase – 'What are the cost implications?' – signified more than they had thought. They had assumed that the preferred option would be identified on technical grounds, and that what they then had to do was to cost only the development and implementation of that one option. Because even that task was quite a challenge in the limited time available, they had not conceived that the client would require cost information for the other options too. If the specification had been thought through in detail and phrased more carefully (and at somewhat greater length!), and if the consultants had asked for confirmation of their assumptions, there might have been less room for misinterpretation.

Over the ensuing weeks, a further exchange of correspondence brought the content of the report closer in line with the MD's expectations. The consultants' report was accepted and their invoice approved for payment. It later transpired that the requirement to cost every option was a point insisted on by the company's board, which had not been given an opportunity to see the work specification.

5

How do I select the right people?

When it comes to choosing a consultant or adviser, the best guide is experience – either your own or that of people whose judgement you trust. If there are individuals or firms that you have used in the past for similar work, you will know whether you are prepared to use them again. Your business may maintain a list of approved or preferred consultants who have supplied evidence of their skills, experience and financial status and who meet required technical and quality standards. Lists and registers of consultants are used by almost all public sector authorities. Figure 5.1 shows a typical format for recording data on a register of consultants.

In the course of their marketing activity, consultants may approach you directly to tell you about the services they offer and try to convince you about the benefits they can bring to your business. If what they have to say matches your situation, you may at least want to keep their details on file. If you get the feeling that it is part of a cold-calling campaign to drum up work from all and sundry, you would be well advised to think twice about following up their approach and instead seek a more informed source of guidance.

CONSULTANT INFORMATION		
Ref No.		
Name of consultant/practice		
....		
Address (main office)		
....		
Phone	Fax	E-mail
....	....	....
Contacts:		
....		

PERSONNEL

Numbers of staff by discipline (A–D)

	A	B	C	D	Specialist skills
Principals		....			....
Associates		....			....
Assistants		....			....

WORK EXPERIENCE

Sectors of experience	Types of work	Approx. current workload (fee values of committed contracts)
A		
B		
C		
D		
E		
F		
G		
H		

CURRENT QUALITY ASSESSMENT (grade A to C with +/? if necessary)

Pre-contract ......   Contract ....   Post-contract ....

Cost control ......   Output delivery ......   General contract performance ......

Employing/task manager(s)

....

....

COMMENTS

Date of initial entry .... Updated (date)...........................

by ....

Figure 5.1 *Example of a consultant register format*

A consultant who has helped you in one area of expertise may be able to refer you to a dependable colleague working in another field. People in your personal or business network may recommend consultants whom they have found efficient and reliable. Other sources of information include professional institutions, many of which maintain referral schemes, directories, trade associations and support organizations working with small businesses and the voluntary sector.

Be mindful, though, that businesses and individuals sometimes set up arrangements under which they are paid a finder's fee or commission for every client they refer to a particular adviser. The fee is, of course, absorbed within the client's bill. The practice is not unlawful or improper, and it is normal in fields such as financial advice. Where a commission payment is made, the adviser ought to disclose this fact to the client, as well as indicating the amount paid for the referral. If you are concerned about the possibility that your referral may have been part of such an arrangement, ask the adviser directly.

Many professional and technical journals include columns in which consultants advertise their services. Internet searches can yield the names of firms and individuals practising in a particular area of specialization, but they should be relied on only to obtain contact addresses, since the impression of a firm made by its Web site may be deceptive. Brochures and other promotional literature should not be taken wholly at face value. The problem with many brochures is that, even when up to date, they are either so generalized and bland as to be uninformative or so generous with fine words that they are mean with facts.

What to look for in a brochure

- Facts about contracts and clients: ignore slick copywriting or glossy pictures.

- Evidence of endorsement from other clients.

- A clear statement of professional purpose.

- Qualities that differentiate the firm and add value to its services.

- Awareness of clients' requirements: 'how we respond to your needs' not 'what we offer'.

- A sense of creativity, innovation and insight.

A brochure is a marketing document; a proposal, as discussed later in this chapter, is a sales document. What is the difference? We can find the answer in a supermarket. Let's say you make food products. A brochure is like the information you give the store buyers to persuade them to stock your products on their shelves. A proposal is like the information on the packaging that persuades the shopper to pick your product off the shelf rather than a competing brand.

Brochures succeed when they market consultancy services intelligently, but on their own they are rarely an effective vehicle for winning work. Proposals that read like brochures usually fail, because they address the market in general instead of focusing on the needs of the specific client.

Try to identify at least three consultants to approach. Look for appropriate credentials and qualifications, but don't necessarily be impressed by strings of letters after people's names (Chapter 2). It's their practical experience and their ability to satisfy your requirements that count. You may find there are people who combine expertise in the work that you need with experience of working for people like yourself or for businesses in your sector. If not, you may have to decide which of these two aspects is the more important.

When you get in touch with the consultants, make it clear that you want to talk either to the owner of the firm or to a principal who can take business decisions. Give them an outline of the work you require and some details about yourself and your organization. Ask if they might be available to help you and if they would be interested in hearing more about the work (Figure 5.2), but explain that you are approaching them without making any commitment.

TAKING UP REFERENCES

Unless you know the consultants too well to require this, ask at the same time for a list of their current and recent clients – specifically, the names of individuals they have worked for or client managers who have been responsible for employing them. Follow up these references at the start, so that you don't waste time dealing with consultants who have a habit of disappointing their clients. It is a mistake to regard

Dear Mr Wilson

The Consultancy Office of the Institute of Business Editors has suggested that you may be able to assist us in a consultancy assignment to develop an improved style and structure for our next Annual Review, due to be published in May, and act as its coordinator and editor.

I am enclosing with this letter a copy of last year's Review, which was produced in-house and which I feel lacks the quality and thrust we should be seeking to communicate in our corporate literature.

If you are interested, please let me know right away – a phone call will suffice – and send me a brief outline of how you would propose to go about the job, how you would see yourself working with the staff of this company, and what you believe are the most useful changes you could make in the style and presentation of the Review. I would find it helpful also to have information about your experience in corporate report production and your availability over the period to May, together with an estimate of the time input the work is likely to require and an estimate of your fees for the work.

We do not want you to go to any great expense, and so I am asking that your proposal should be with me by the end of next week. The proposal should be brief, ideally no more than four or five pages long.

I should point out that I am also writing in the same terms to two other consultants.

Please contact me by phone if there are any points you would like to discuss.

Yours sincerely

John Smith

The letter is to the point and does its job effectively, but there are questions left unanswered. The consultant who received it needed to get on the phone quickly to arrange to meet the client and try to obtain a better understanding of the company so as to be able to put in a workable proposal.

Figure 5.2 _Example of a client's letter of inquiry_

taking up references as something you do just to help confirm your choice.

Ask consultants to identify the persons who engaged or worked with them: the names of organizations on their own are not enough. Pick out two or three names – other private individuals or organizations like yours (though not direct business competitors!) – to contact for references about the consultants. A simple phone conversation should be all that is necessary: people are generally more forthcoming on the phone than when asked to write down their views.

The key points to determine are whether the consultants can be relied on to do a good job, what they are like to work with and whether the people you are talking to would use them again. You may want to ask specific questions about technical competence, delivery, value for money, working relationships and other factors. In certain litigious environments some clients may be reluctant to express themselves freely about consultants; but if consultants are hesitant to give you information about their clients or claim the information is commercially confidential, be on your guard.

Of course, some consultants may volunteer the names of people with whom they have personal or business connections, so you may not always get an unbiased view. You have to rely on instinct to tell you if a response seems genuine.

FOLLOW-UP MEETING

Consultants will probably want to talk to you and explore your needs in more detail before responding. You too are likely to see advantages in meeting them face to face. It is reasonable to expect the consultant not to charge for this meeting: check beforehand that this is the case.

Try to arrange to meet them on their home ground. Does their office look welcoming and well organized or is it a shambles? Do staff look under stress or do they seem to be going about their work in a focused and purposeful manner? Remember that consultants may try to stage-manage your visit (Chapter 2). Do not assume that a consultant who works from home is any less competent to fulfil your needs than a firm with a corporate office; but working from home should not mean working amid a chaos of domestic clutter.

You will find it useful if they can give some prior thought to your requirements. Ahead of the meeting, send them either a copy of the work specification or a summary that emphasizes the points you regard as critical to the success of the work. Before it goes to them, check that it is accurate and consistent, and take out any points or comments that should be kept to yourself.

While you are sizing up the people you might be working with, bear in mind that they will be doing the same. Consultants will be trying to assess whether your intentions are serious, whether you are just sounding out the market or trawling for ideas, whether what you want them to achieve is realistic and – not least – whether you are likely to be able to pay their bills. In some cases they may ask you to complete a questionnaire so as to form a profile of you as a client. They may decline your business if they feel the assignment would expose them to risk or a conflict of interest, or if they sense that, for personal or commercial motives, you might expect them to compromise their professional judgement (Chapter 1).

Take notes during the meeting and then try to form an overall view of the consultants' response. The following points may be useful in giving you a feel for their attitude and competence:

- Are the consultants good listeners? Are they attentive to what you have to say or do they spend the time telling you how good they are? And are they good communicators – do they talk in terms you can understand?

- Do they have a down-to-earth, common-sense attitude?

- Do they seem efficient, businesslike and enthusiastic about the prospect of working for you?

- What experience do they have in carrying out similar work to the job you have in mind?

- Do they show an insight into your situation? Are they pointing out things you hadn't thought of, and are they prepared to say, 'We don't know the answer to that question, but we will find out'?

- Can they confirm their ability to undertake the work in the required timescale?

- Can they say who exactly would be dealing with your work? Would they be doing it all themselves, or would they need to bring in others?

- If the meeting is with a firm of consultants rather than an individual practitioner, who are the owners of the firm?

- How do they normally charge for their services, and what are their average costs for the type of work you require? Are they open and forthcoming about their fees?

- Are they working for a business competitor?

- How do they assure quality and value for money?

- Do they have any necessary professional indemnity cover?

- Is there an opportunity to see the results of their work? For example, can they show you copies of reports they have produced for other clients?

- Do you feel comfortable with them? Can you form a good working relationship?

- Do you feel you can trust them to act in your best interests?

If all this makes choosing a consultant seem like a task to be gone through methodically after careful thought, well, that is the intention. There are consultants who believe that the golf course and the clubhouse are the best places to win work (what one source in the construction industry has called 'the gregarious, alcohol-fuelled realities of schmoozing clients'). It is true that in some fields contracts can be won with rounds of whisky, but do you really think it sensible to let your judgement be manipulated in that way?

It may be evident just from these meetings that there is one consultant who can match your requirements more effectively or offer better value for money than any other. If so, all that is needed is a simple exchange of letters. But before you write to the consultant, make sure that you have identified clearly the work you want done and that the consultant has quoted you a firm price for the work. Confirm these points when letting the consultant know that you intend to use his or her services (Figure 5.3).

In reply, some consultants may send you standard terms of engagement reflecting the requirements or advice of their professional institutions (Figure 5.4 and Figure 5.16 at the end of this chapter) and ask you to confirm your acceptance of those terms. Points to watch out for in dealing with terms of engagement are discussed in Chapter 6.

Once you have agreed terms with your chosen consultant, let the others know they were unsuccessful, and do it straight away. That should be one of the normal courtesies of business. It is not only unhelpful to consultants to be contacted by a potential client and then hear nothing further, but you are unlikely to get a keen response should you ever need to approach them again.

Dear Mr Wilson

I enjoyed our meeting at your offices last Thursday. I thought we had a useful discussion, and as a result I am glad to let you know that my company intends to commission you to undertake the development, coordination and editorial work for the forthcoming 2004 Annual Review.

The scope of the commission will be as discussed at the meeting and outlined in the Attachment to this letter.

The Review has to be circulated to our stakeholders by 31 May. On the understanding that you will be able to start work on the commission immediately, our board will wish to have your initial ideas on the style and structure of the Review by the end of February, and your proposals for text contributions and graphics will need to be ready no more than six weeks later, ie by mid-April.

Your time estimate of 25 working days' input and your proposed inclusive rate of £500 per day net of VAT are acceptable to the company, subject to valuation. The work will have a budget ceiling of £12,500.

You will shortly receive from me a form of contract, which I trust will be in line with our previous discussions and with the terms recommended by your professional institute. In the meantime, if you have questions about any of the points in this letter, please let me know.

I look forward to our working together on this project.

Yours sincerely

John Smith

Figure 5.3 _Example of a client's letter of intent_

SEEKING MORE INFORMATION

If you are unable to reach a rapid decision and feel the need for more information, the simplest course is to ask consultants to come for an interview or to make a brief presentation. Let consultants know how much time will be available for the interview and who should attend: it is the person or people who would do the work and manage the process that you need to see, not a high-flying director or a business development manager from their head office.

Dear Mr Jones

When we met on 25 June, you asked me to indicate how I might be able to assist you in the preparation and submission of a planning application. This letter outlines my ideas on the scope and programme of the work, and sets out an estimate of the costs involved.

In undertaking the work, I would expect to perform the following tasks:

- visiting the site;

- appraising relevant planning policies;

- preparing a draft application, including illustrative material;

- meeting local planning authority officers to discuss the scheme prior to submission;

- submitting the application and monitoring its progress.

The work would be undertaken by my Senior Assistant, Miss Jane Smith, who is a Member of the Royal Town Planning Institute.

I estimate that the work will require an input of 20 working days and will be completed by 16 August.

The fee for this work would be charged on a time-spent basis, net of VAT and expenses, with the latter reimbursable at cost. I enclose a copy of my firm's current schedule of daily rates, and our standard terms of engagement. On the basis of 20 days' input, the estimated fee will be in the order of £8,000 net of VAT and expenses. I am annexing to this letter a note that details the basis of this estimate.

Should you require additional work to be undertaken that is not covered by the tasks listed above, I would be pleased to provide an estimate in respect of the costs of such additional work.

I would propose to invoice you on completion of the work.

I would be grateful to receive your written confirmation that the terms of this proposal are acceptable. Please let me know if you wish me to provide more information on any point. I look forward to hearing from you in due course.

Yours sincerely

Figure 5.4 *Example of a consultant's letter of agreement (based on Starting in Private Practice, Royal Town Planning Institute, 2001)*

As an agenda, draw up a list of questions that cover your requirements and concerns, but this time don't let the people you are interviewing see it in advance. If they want to give a PowerPoint presentation and you have projection facilities in your office, all well and good, but do not incur any costs on their behalf. Their approach to the presentation and the quality of its delivery should tell you how practical they are likely to be as advisers.

When judging a presentation, consider the following points:

- How did the consultants respond to your questions? Did they give straight answers or were they evasive or uncertain?

- Were they focused on your requirements or did they spend the time talking about their services, their achievements and their credentials?

- Did they come over as intelligent, confident and eager to do the work?

- Did you take to them as people?

- Was the presentation enjoyable or a bore?

- Did it look flashy and overburdened with visual effects? That may indicate a lack of substance.

In other situations – particularly where you are concerned about the approach and methods that a consultant is likely to adopt – you may ask the consultant to send you a proposal detailing his or her response to your work specification together with information about resources, costs and so forth. Make it clear that your decision on appointing the consultant will depend on your analysis of the proposal.

Old hands v new faces

Let's suppose there is work you need done, and you have consultants working for you now or whom you engaged in the recent past who could do it. Should you give them this further work? If it is a sequel to their previous contract and you are reasonably satisfied with their past performance, they may well be the right choice. You will know their people and their strengths, and they in turn will be familiar with your requirements and priorities. There will be no steep learning curve to face, which should result

---

in less exposure to risk than would be presented by new consultants. All this means that you are likely to be more comfortable with consultants you know. But comfort can at times slide into an over-friendly and cosy relationship in which clients develop a long-term dependence on one firm that then takes for granted its entrenchment and continuing employment. Clients grow complacent, and consultants become stale. If you recognize this situation, it is time for a change.

New consultants will need to get up to speed about the way your business operates and what you expect in terms of performance and delivery, but they can be a source of new ideas as well as offering a fresh and energetic approach. Their staff may be just as skilled and resourceful as your existing consultants, and if they are a younger and smaller firm they will probably carry a lesser burden of overheads and so may be able to quote a keener price for the work.

There are three key questions to consider:

■ Who are likely to give you better value for money – your existing consultants or new ones?

■ Would a change of consultants bring practical benefits in terms of service quality and results?
■ Are you likely to secure a more constructive working relationship with new consultants?

The best way to answer these questions may be to put the work out to competition, inviting bids from existing and new consultants and comparing their responses. Points to look for when evaluating proposals from existing consultants are discussed later in this chapter.

Case Study

Following a series of mergers and acquisitions, the company – part of an investment group that specialized in sports and leisure complexes – appointed a new business development manager. She came from another company in the group where her project management role had involved working with consultants and advisers from a range of engineering disciplines. She considered herself a shrewd judge of competence and value for money where consultants were concerned.

At her new company, she found that she had inherited the presence of a firm of environmental engineers who had been its consultants for at least a dozen years. They had a long record of repeat work, commissioned largely by technical managers who had come to see them as a virtually indispensable bank of resources: no other firm of consultants could muster a team of engineers who knew so much about the way the company worked. Why, some of their senior consultants had even been managers in the company.

She did not know the firm in question. At her initial meetings with them she sensed they regarded themselves very much as sitting tenants who had almost a right to the work that came their way. The company's procurement staff shared her concerns about the consultants. They were unhappy with the high rates the firm charged, did not believe it gave good value for money, and were uneasy about the personal links between its management and the company.

The consultants completed one assignment for her, but there were problems about their performance and she did not like their business approach or take to them as people. Market testing confirmed that the expertise needed by the company could be obtained from other, smaller firms of environmental engineers. When the next large contract came up for tendering, the company chose to manage the project with an in-house team and split the technical work into several packages that went to a number of the smaller firms. It reckoned that the benefits gained through access to a broader range of approaches and ideas outweighed the increased costs of tendering, administration and contract monitoring.

For their part, the consultants acknowledged that they had failed to appreciate the vulnerability of their position as a consequence of the changes in the client's head office: they had rashly assumed their record of experience meant that they did not have to prove themselves to the new manager.

GOING OUT TO TENDER

We are all familiar with the principle of getting quotations from two or three tradespeople for work that may need to be done around the house. Inviting bids from consultants need not be much more complicated than that. If you want to make sure you identify the consultant most likely to deliver the best results and the best value for money, and if making the wrong choice of consultant could place you or your business at risk, you need a procedure that is somewhat more formal than the one described so far. This means putting the work out to competitive bidding (Figure 5.5) – inviting written offers in which consultants set out their approach, work plan, resources, costs and other information.

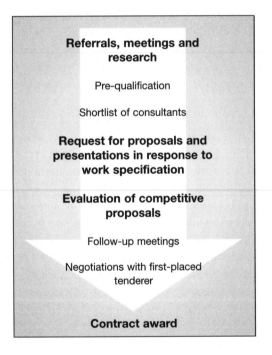

Referrals, meetings and research

Pre-qualification

Shortlist of consultants

Request for proposals and presentations in response to work specification

Evaluation of competitive proposals

Follow-up meetings

Negotiations with first-placed tenderer

Contract award

Figure 5.5 *Outline of the competitive tendering process*

Figure 5.6 shows a procurement structure that is characteristic of business units in large companies. There are three main participants: 1) the manager responsible for the tendering process, for commissioning the work, running the client's side of the contract and maintaining the day-to-day working relationship with the consultant; 2) a procurement manager who assists the business unit manager in dealing with contractual matters; and 3) technical specialists who can advise the business unit manager about detailed aspects of the work.

Putting work out to tender does not necessarily involve a mass of documentation or complex procedures – at least, not in the private sector. The information you require from consultants by way of an offer should be in proportion to the scale and challenge of the work, and a simple form of quotation may be sufficient. The form shown in Figure 5.7 offers a useful model: the client fills in Section A and sends a copy to the consultants, who complete Section B and return the form to the client.

Writing a proposal is a more time-consuming task than sending in a quotation and can prove expensive for consultants. You too will have to spend time setting out the information that will enable consultants to respond adequately to your request, and you will then have to invest even more time and effort in examining and comparing the competing proposals.

In some circumstances, particularly when the technical quality of the outcome is likely to be no less decisive than its costs, it may be useful to structure the bidding procedure into stages. At its simplest, there may be two: first, a stage of pre-qualification, when you narrow the field down to a shortlist of consultants best qualified to undertake the work; second, a tendering stage, when you receive and evaluate submissions from the shortlisted firms.

Figure 5.8 offers points of guidance on pre-qualification. For complex, high-value and high-risk contracts, you may want to extend the bidding procedure into what is termed a 'competitive dialogue', discussing your requirements with selected consultants through successive stages of analysis until you have identified the most promising solution. The consultants are then invited to submit final proposals addressing that solution.

Business unit manager

- Justifies need for use of consultants
- Obtains authority to procure consultancy services and set up a trading agreement
- Prepares a detailed work specification
- Agrees selection criteria for proposal list and evaluation criteria
- Evaluates proposals and recommends contract award
- Administers consultancy contract
- Administers change control, variation control and fee accounts
- Prepares periodic cost reports and cash flow forecasts
- Processes invoices for payment
- Coordinates, monitors and evaluates the work of the consultants
- Administers close-out of the consultancy contract

Procurement manager

- Develops consultancy market knowledge
- Forecasts and plans consultancy requirements
- Develops optimum sourcing and contracting strategies
- Assesses abilities and resources of consultants
- Maintains lists of approved/preferred consultants
- Processes requests for consultancy services
- Undertakes appointment process for consultancy services
- Monitors liabilities and processing of payments and fee accounts
- Collates performance data, analyzes and records results
- Provides feedback to consultants and supply chain partners

Technical specialists

- Advise on work specification
- Advise on health and safety, quality assurance, environment, legal issues
- Advise on selection and evaluation criteria
- Participate in evaluation of proposals

Figure 5.6 *Typical procurement structure*

INVITING PROPOSALS

The tasks involved on your part in preparing a work specification and on the consultants' part in developing a proposal have sufficient parallels as to be virtually reflections of each other. Inviting competitive proposals brings a range of benefits, including access to different ideas, approaches and solutions and a chance to judge the professional chemistry likely to develop between you and the consultants. The proposal is in large measure a proxy for the performance of the work.

SECTION A   CLIENT SPECIFICATION
Scope of work and outputs required   Ref no......................
Specific requirements
Deliverables and delivery dates
Timescale   Earliest start date............................   Latest completion date........................

Contract basis   ☐ Fixed price
                          ☐ Time charges
                          ☐ Other (specify)

Budget information (where applicable)
Payment terms
Task Manager (*name, signature, date*)   ....

SECTION B   CONSULTANT RESPONSE
Consultant (*name, address, contact data*)   Authorized signatory...
Observations on client specification (*Continue on separate sheet if necessary.*)
Estimate of charge for the services specified in Section A   (*Itemize on separate sheet if necessary.*)   Fixed price   Time charges   Fee..........................   Fees...   Expenses....................   (*Detail time rates as appropriate.*)   (*where appropriate*)   Expenses..   **Total estimated charge** ....   The consultant offers to provide services in accordance with Section A for the above total estimated charge.   Signed.. Date........................

Figure 5.7 *Example of a simple form of quotation*

Pre-qualification is much more common in public sector procurement than in private sector contracting. Businesses are likely to find the procedure useful and cost-effective only when they are dealing with large contracts, when the opportunity for consultancy services has been advertised in the technical press and when a sizeable response is expected. Through pre-qualification, clients can make sure that they invite proposals only from the firms or individuals whose skills and experience most closely match the requirements of the work.

Consultants and advisers are normally invited to pre-qualify for a contract by submitting expressions of interest or completing pre-qualification forms. The use of standardized forms helps clients obtain a consistent basis for comparing and assessing information.

Pre-qualification information required by clients normally covers at least the following topics:

- **Corporate data:**
  - the business status of the consultant or adviser;
  - office and contact details.
- **Experience, skills and performance:**
  - specialist skills and competencies;
  - quality accreditation;
  - a list of comparable work assignments completed;
  - contract performance record – specifically any failure to complete a contract or termination by a client, with an explanation of the reasons;
  - current work commitments, with names of clients.
- **Resources:**
  - details of current staff, including CVs of key personnel;
  - charge rate information for key personnel;
  - specialist resources and facilities, eg IT, laboratories, training;
  - professional indemnity and other insurances.
- **Financial status:**
  - bank references;
  - published or certified accounts for the last two/three years of trading, plus a copy of the latest management accounts.

Evidence you should look for in assessing this information:

- the skills and resources needed to deliver your work successfully;
- a good track record in similar work: look for facts, client references, dates and contract values;
- financial health: does the consultant appear likely to remain in business over and beyond the lifetime of the contract?

Has the consultant supplied all the information you asked for?

Is the information focused on areas of expertise and experience relevant to your work?

Figure 5.8 *Guidance on pre-qualification*

It is the closest that consultants normally get to providing you with a free sample. The quality of the proposals will, in most instances, give you a reliable indication of the quality of work you can expect from the consultants and the value they can add to your business.

It is up to you to say what information should go in the proposal, what its structure should be and how it should be set out. If you leave these matters to the consultants, you will be faced with an 'apples and oranges' situation. Each proposal will answer your request for information in a different way – for example, with prices expressed in widely divergent terms – and you will find it hard to make any useful comparison between them. It is safer to give consultants a structure to follow so as to secure a consistent basis on which to evaluate their responses.

The information required in a consultant's proposal will depend on the character of each assignment but normally it will include the following items:

- Information about the individual, firm or group submitting the proposal.

- Their background and experience, including details of recent and comparable work.

- Their understanding of your objectives and requirements.

- Their proposed work programme or delivery plan in response to your requirements – what they undertake to deliver and when – and the technical methods and procedures they would apply to the work.

- The timescale in which they would undertake the work, with an estimate of the total time to be spent on the work.

- Their proposed arrangements for organizing and managing the work.

- The price they propose to charge and the elements that make up their price (Chapter 3). You need this information in a form that will allow you to make direct cost comparisons. Ask them to provide an overall, bottom-line cost and the price of specific deliverables. If the work has distinct parts or components, ask them to cost these separately.

■ How they propose to resource the work, ie information about the people who would work on your assignment. Since the outcome of the work will depend largely on their efforts, energies and skills, you may need to have them identified individually in the proposal, with CVs that relate their qualifications and competencies to their work responsibilities. In some contexts – for example, where the assignment involves a number of teams and work units – it may be sufficient to require details only of the core members or leaders of each team.

■ Details of any subcontractors they may intend to use.

The items in this list are the minimum information you would expect to see in any proposal. You may well want the consultants to include information on other points that reflect specific features of the work or particular concerns on your part. For example, you might ask them to include a quality assurance plan or to describe their approach to management communication, resource scheduling (including, perhaps, a bar chart of staff inputs), progress measurement, performance monitoring and risk sharing.

Before finalizing the proposal requirements, look again at the work specification to make sure it mirrors accurately your current view of your priorities. Refresh the thinking that went into it and if necessary revise and amend its terms to bring it up to date. Check through your analysis of the work, your assessment of its practical demands and your reasons for enlisting outside help, to make sure you have covered all the relevant items. Rid the text of any internal management jargon or unexplained acronyms.

As well as sending them the work specification (Chapter 4), you will need to give consultants clear directions about the way you want them to present their proposals. It goes without saying that each of them should receive exactly the same information from you. The points to communicate include the following requirements.

How the proposal is to be submitted

■ First of all, make it absolutely clear who is issuing the invitation to tender – ie you, your company, your business unit or an organization that you represent.

- Details of the information or enclosures accompanying your letter of invitation – for example, the work specification (if it is a separate document), data sheets, statistical material or a draft contract.

- The format in which the proposal should be submitted – for example, as a letter, a set of completed forms, an e-mail attachment or files on a floppy disk or CD. Make it clear if a particular form of submission is not acceptable: for example, you may wish to veto submissions by fax, since these can monopolize your phone lines.

- Any limit you may want to set on the size of the proposal or the number of pages devoted to particular items: for example, 'no more than 10 A4 sides' or 'each CV shall be no more than two pages in length'. The shorter the proposals, the easier it ought to be to manage their evaluation.

- Any requirements you may have about the way in which particular categories of information are presented. For example, you may want price information to be set out in a specific style or format. If so, include a template within your documentation – say, in the form of an Excel worksheet – and make it clear that consultants are expected to conform to it. As examples, Figures 5.9 and 5.10 show templates that can be used to obtain CV information and work record information respectively in a consistent format.

- The number of copies required.

- Any documents that need to accompany the proposal: for example, copies of current insurance certificates, company articles of association, details of suppliers who can provide trade references, and so forth.

- The deadline for receipt of the proposal. Don't make this unnecessarily tight. Allow enough time for the consultants to prepare a full and informed response. Rushing the proposal stage will cause problems later on.

- The address to which the proposal should be sent.

- The person for whose attention it should be marked.

- Any requirements you may have about the packaging or labelling of the proposal: for example, you may want the outer package or envelope containing the proposal to carry no indication of the consultants' identity.

Name:

Profession:

Fields of specialization:

Proposed role/position:

Year of birth:	Years with firm:	Nationality:

Key qualifications:
(Give a summary of professional strengths – outlining experience, extent of responsibilities, professional achievements, expertise in specialized fields, knowledge of a particular technology or environment.)

Education and professional status:
(List professional affiliations, diplomas, degrees, scholarships, awards and distinctions, vocational certificates, specialized courses and training.)

Record of recent experience:
(In reverse chronological order, list recent experience relevant to the contract, indicating the employment held, activities undertaken and responsibilities fulfilled.)

Computer experience (where appropriate):
(Indicate knowledge of operating systems, applications, databases, programming, software development and experience of a support environment.)

Language ability (where appropriate):
(Indicate grades of proficiency in speaking, reading and writing.)

Publications (where appropriate):

(Other categories of information relevant to specialized fields):

Certification:

I, the undersigned, certify that to the best of my knowledge and belief the data given here correctly describe myself, my qualifications and my experience.

Signature .... Date ....

Figure 5.9 *Example of a template for CV information*

Name of assignment:	Client/client organization:
Location and description of assignment:	

Description of actual services provided by your firm:	Name of client manager:
	Client address and contact data (phone/fax/e-mail):
Start date:	Completion date:

Key staff engaged on the assignment, indicating functions and responsibilities:

Approx. value of services:

Certification:

I, the undersigned, certify that to the best of my knowledge and belief the data given here are correct.

Signature .... Date ....

Post ....

Figure 5.10 *Example of a template for work record information*

■ Whether you require an immediate acknowledgement of receipt of the invitation and a statement of the consultants' intention to submit a proposal.

Contact information

- The person to contact if there are questions or points that need clarification (see below).

- Whether you want the consultants to meet you for a discussion before submitting their proposal.

How the proposal is to be structured

- The items of information required in the proposal, and how they should be set out – for example, as sections dealing with particular topics or as a set of forms. When listing the required content, perhaps introduce it with a phrase such as, 'A complete response to the request for a proposal must include. . .'.

- Encouragement to keep the proposal to the point, eg by not including brochure material.

- Whether proposals that do not conform in full to the work specification will be rejected, and if not the extent to which departures will be allowed.

- Any requirement to show quality accreditation or to demonstrate compliance with regulations in fields appropriate to the work – for example, health and safety and environmental legislation.

- Any requirement to provide details, including contact names and addresses, of clients for whom the consultants have undertaken comparable services under contract within, say, the last two or three years.

Figure 5.11 outlines a typical structure that accommodates the basic categories of information required in most proposals. You might ask consultants to complete a response matrix on the lines illustrated in Figure 5.12. This is a counterpart of the compliance matrix widely used in procurement for goods and supplies. It lists the items and requirements set out in the work specification and asks consultants to indicate where these points are addressed in their proposals. Using this type of matrix has two advantages for you: 1) it provides a checklist to help confirm whether the consultants have addressed all your requirements; 2) it guides you directly to specific items of information – you do not

Introductory section

explaining
- Purpose of the proposal
- Key benefits offered by the proposal
- Professional resources and experience of the consultants

Approach and methodology

explaining
- The consultants' understanding of the client's objectives
- Work method
- Tasks and activities needed to achieve the intended results

Work plan and timetable

explaining
- Timing of professional inputs
- Proposed arrangements for managing the work

Staffing

explaining
- Personnel to be used on the work
- Responsibilities

Outputs and deliverables

explaining
- Items or services to be provided to the client

Team and contract experience

including
- CVs of personnel
- Summaries of experience on similar contracts

Price information

setting out
- Estimates of costs (fees and expenses)

Figure 5.11 *Typical proposal structure*

have to spend time hunting them down in the text, and so the task of evaluating proposals becomes easier.

What inputs you will provide to the work

These were discussed in Chapter 4 and may include premises, equipment

Item	Work specification reference (clause/paragraph)	Proposal reference (clause/paragraph)	Proposal page reference
Objectives	1.1		
Scope of the work	1.2–1.5		
Approach and method	1.6–1.8		
Required skills and competencies	1.9–1.10		
Task A	1.11		
Task B	1.12		
Task C	1.13		
Task D	1.14		
Specific procedures	1.15–1.16		
Quality management	1.17		
Progress and performance monitoring	1.18		
Timetable	1.19, Figure 1.1		
Detailed work plan and programme	1.20–1.21		
Schedule of deliverables	1.22		
Inputs	1.23–1.24		

Figure 5.12 *Detail of a response matrix*

and materials as well as data, access to offices and staff and logistical support.

Your expectations about resources and performance

Provide whatever guidance you feel appropriate about the number of people you would expect to do the work and the competencies you want them to possess. If the work will require the attention of a team of consultants, make clear any requirement to include in the team particular individuals who are recognized authorities in their fields, or to involve particular sources of expertise, such as a named research centre or university department. Indicate any requirements for individuals to hold specific qualifications, insurances or licences.

Because the capability, personality and experience of the team leader can play so critical a part in the way the work is performed, it is in your interests to specify with particular care the responsibilities that go with this post. The terms in which you define the team leader's functions will significantly affect your capacity to reduce the project's level of exposure to risk from the resource and management problems outlined in Chapter 4.

Require information about the experience of the individuals who would be doing the work, and particularly the success they have achieved with other clients. It is their experience that counts, not the status and reputation of the firm employing them. Make sure that these individuals are identified in the proposal. You do not want to find yourself paying senior prices for junior expertise.

Say whether you expect all the persons engaged on your work to be on the permanent staff of the consultants submitting the proposal, rather than freelance or self-employed individuals brought in from outside. The case for preferring to use permanent staff rests on several points:

- If they have maintained a place on the firm's payroll, they may seem to offer an assurance of quality.

- The management and coordination of their inputs may appear more secure.

- They may ensure a closer match to your competence requirements: a firm can be expected to be familiar with the temperament and aptitudes of staff members, and should know how well they would fit into a particular work environment.

- They may be better motivated than freelance staff and less inclined to set their own priorities in terms of working hours and commitment, as well as less likely to depart to other employment.

On the other hand, there are many firms that operate with only a small body of full-time personnel and rely on outside advisers to staff their assignments. Some highly specialized areas of knowledge may be accessible only through experts working on their own account. One way of acknowledging these characteristics is to allow firms to offer freelance experts who have an established consultancy relationship with them.

Identify any project management programmes that you will require the consultants to apply in resourcing and controlling their side of the work and reporting progress on project activities. You may, for example, want to be able to coordinate their management reports (Chapter 7) with your own systems for recording inputs, monitoring progress, controlling costs and analysing efficiency.

If it is critical that deadlines are met, state that time will be of the essence in performing the contract. This tells the consultants that you will hold them liable if results are delayed owing to factors within their control.

Specify that the firms and individuals forming the consultant team shall not be either engaged in work or intending to work during the proposed contract period for clients whose interests are opposed to or incompatible with your own, such as business competitors.

VIEWPOINT

'Much of the work we commission has to do with sizeable development projects, where a single firm of consultants just will not have the full range of expertise that is needed. So we generally enlist a consortium of firms. One problem we find with the legal and financial consultants in a consortium is that they tend to come to the work with an entrenched solution. It's like the familiar cliché, "If the only tool you have is a hammer, everything looks like a nail." Our projects are not designed for standard solutions. We need flexibility and the versatility that enables people to explore different avenues and approaches.

'Our consultants are likely to have to appear on our behalf at inquiries and appeals. So we cannot afford to make the wrong choice. It is essential that we choose firms with principals who can lead on the evidence effectively and give a solid, confident performance when cross-examined.'

(Director of a property development group)

Contract-related information

Include the following points:

- The type of contract that you have in mind for the work – for example, whether it will be based on a fixed price or on time inputs (Chapter 6).

- The final output or deliverable that will signify completion of the work. This will often take the form of a report or presentation. When defining this item, use a phrase such as 'approved final report' or 'agreed presentation', and make it clear that you will need to be satisfied with it, as well as all other outputs specified under the contract, before the work can be considered to have been completed.

- The expected duration of the contract or the work – in terms of either time span or output: for example, 'the duration of the contract will extend until satisfactory completion of the final report, which shall not be later than. . .'.

- The criteria you intend to apply in evaluating the proposals.

- Whether a follow-up presentation will be required.

- The date by which you expect to have reached a decision about the outcome of the tendering process.

- Whether you are prepared to accept modifications to your work specification or what is termed a 'variant solution'. Consultants may put this forward as a means of meeting your requirements more effectively than the course of action outlined in the work specification, and it may offer a more informed approach. If modifications and variant solutions are not acceptable, make that clear.

- Indicate how long you want the proposal – and in particular the price information – to remain valid. In defining this point, make a realistic assessment of the time likely to be needed for proposal evaluation and subsequent contractual negotiations. It is not uncommon for clients to require a price to hold good for, say, 90 days.

- Whether you have included in the documentation a Form of Tender that consultants are required to complete in order to indicate that they accept the scope of work and the conditions defined by you either in a draft contract or in the work specification (Figure 5.13).

- Some consultants may misinterpret your invitation to bid as evidence of an intention to sign a contract with them. Safeguard your position by stating that the invitation is part of a competitive tendering procedure, that the contract will be awarded on the basis of your assessment of value for money and that you reserve the right not to accept the lowest-priced or any tender.

Form of Tender

To:

Contracts and Finance Manager
ABC Ltd

Dear Sir/Madam

We the undersigned hereby offer to provide consultancy services as set out in Schedule 1 (Scope of work) at the prices detailed in Schedule 2 (Price information).

We certify that this is a bona fide tender, that we have not communicated to any person other than the Company the amount or approximate amount of the tender price and that such price has not been fixed or adjusted by arrangement or in collusion with any third party.

All prices stated in this tender are firm fixed prices not subject to contract price adjustment or exchange rate fluctuations for the duration of the contract.

Our tender is valid and open for acceptance for 90 days from the date below.

SIGNED:

POSITION:

For and on behalf of: ....

ADDRESS:

DATE:

Figure 5.13 *Example of a Form of Tender*

There are two further points to make clear:

■ First, that you accept no liability for costs incurred either in preparing the proposal or in any subsequent contract negotiations. It is a condition that most clients will wish to impose, though in some professional fields such as advertising, marketing and industrial design, where the costs of preparing proposals and presentations can be steep, it is not unusual for clients to reimburse consultants for at least part of their expenses. This happens particularly when the client is aware of the effort that consultants normally put into their bids and knows that proposals and presentations are themselves likely to yield benefits in terms of the development and analysis of options and approaches.

■ Second, that the information in the work specification is provided solely for the guidance and convenience of those submitting proposals and that they are expected to make their own investigations to determine the facts of the situation. This is to deter consultants from seeking to make a claim against you if information given in the work specification turns out to have been incorrect. In some jurisdictions there is case law that places a duty on a client organization to disclose to bidders knowledge that it possesses at the time of bidding and that might reasonably have a material effect on the tenders submitted.

Disclosing your budget

Telling consultants how much you can spend? That sounds like an invitation not to tender but to take you to the cleaners. Why on earth would you want to do that? Well, being told your budget will help consultants gauge the level of effort they can realistically put into the work and it is likely to encourage them to focus their proposals on the scale of the benefits they can offer you. It should make it easier for you to identify the proposals that offer real differences in terms of quality and value for money. And it will reduce the risk of receiving proposals that are either unhelpfully out of scale with the funds available for the work or so widely divergent in their costs and proposed inputs as to defy comparability.

There are opposing arguments. Declaring your budget may deprive you of the opportunity to make cost savings. The budget figure will need to be calculated expertly and even then will represent only an indicative sum, which may well need to be revised once the work starts. You may also be concerned that revealing the available budget will encourage consultants to hoist their prices up to the limit. But whatever price they name, they will still have to justify it by demonstrating value for money in terms of the quality of their proposed inputs and the scale of their effort.

While recognizing the advantages of advising consultants about the level of professional effort you expect to see put into the work, you may still be reluctant to make your budget known. Then two other courses are open to you. One is to express your budget as a range within which the costs of the work are expected to fall. The other course is to indicate the length of time or the total number of working days you believe the job should take: this estimate of time should be given only by way of guidance, and your proposal information should make it clear that consultants are free to put forward their own time estimates.

Inviting comments on the work specification

What is perhaps a novel or unfamiliar task to you, like making a planning application or restructuring part of a business, may be a job that consultants do all the time. They can offer new ideas and alternative viewpoints that you might not have considered. Giving them an opportunity to comment on your work specification can be useful to you for several reasons:

- They may draw attention to items that need further consideration when negotiating and agreeing a contract.

- They may offer ideas that can help achieve your objectives more economically, rapidly and dependably.

- The way they comment may give you a feel for the quality of the relationship you would have with them.

Answering questions

Despite your best efforts, there may be points in the work specification and tender documentation that consultants need to ask you to clarify. Give them the opportunity to contact you for more information and be ready to meet them to discuss your requirements in detail. Your contact person should be someone who knows the job well enough to be able to answer questions directly.

Consultants will sometimes use this opportunity to test their ideas on you, to try to gain endorsement for their approach or even to seek your help in putting together a team. 'We're having some difficulty finding a suitable specialist in that field. Do you know of anyone we might approach?' 'What would you think if we went about the job in the following way?' Questions of that sort go further than requests for clarification and may lead you to treat one consultant more favourably than another. Though there is no legal requirement for a business in the private sector to treat all bidders equally and even-handedly, as there is in public sector procurement, you may prefer to keep the competition fair and unbiased. So it may be advisable to limit your answers to matters of fact or the meaning of items in the work specification. Often the best response is simply to say, 'Whatever ideas you have, put them in the proposal. That is what the proposal is for.'

Bids for repeat business

If you already have consultants helping you and are reasonably satisfied with their performance, they are bound to win any tender for a further phase of the work, aren't they? Well, they will certainly be well placed to put in a competent bid, but they have to recognize that they are in competition and they should not expect to be awarded more work as of right. Their bid for the work needs to show an extra dimension that reflects their experience with you, sets them apart from competitors and projects powerful credentials for extending the professional relationship.

Points to look for include:

- Insights that only someone who had worked with you would be able to offer.

- Evidence that they have learnt from experience: if there are aspects of their work that ran into problems, have they addressed these points directly in the bid or skirted round them? What have they done to put things right?

- A clear sense of how they will build on their existing work to give you an even better quality of service.

- A price that is realistic in relation to the required work input, offers productivity savings through knowledge of your working environment and is credible in the light of previous cost levels.

- Individuals whom you know and whose skills have added value to your organization.

- An energetic and enthusiastic response to the work opportunity.

- Signs that they have taken measures to minimize risks and safeguard your objectives.

REACHING A DECISION

Work specifications sometimes fall on barren ground. If none of the consultants you invite cares to put in a bid, you will need to identify why your work was so unappetizing. Don't go straight out to tender again without reconsidering your whole approach. But let's assume that you have followed the advice in Chapter 4, sent out a well-prepared work specification and now have at least one proposal on your desk.

In many instances, all the situation may require is for you to look through each proposal and check that the points that matter to you most have been dealt with, so that you can come to a decision there and then. A second opinion, though, is useful – and involving three people allows at least the possibility of a majority view. The size of the team assessing the proposals and the backgrounds of the persons making the evaluation normally reflect the scale and complexity of the assignment. People taking part need to be competent to gauge the value for money of a proposal and its practicality in terms of methods, resources and programming. Ideally they should have been involved in preparing the work specification and tender documentation. They should not have a financial interest in the decision and ought to declare any potential conflict of interest.

There are circumstances in which it may be useful to engage a consultant specifically to help with the evaluation – for example, if the technical content of the proposals requires specialist analysis or if you feel your decision would benefit from a more informed basis of judgement than is available to you in-house. The advantages you can gain from a consultant include an insider's view of the professionalism and practicality of the proposals: he or she may detect strengths and weaknesses that may not be evident to you. As in the case of consultants assisting with the development of the work specification (Chapter

4), you should choose someone who does not have a personal or business interest in the outcome of the selection process.

Compliance

In the public sector and many areas of industry and commerce, it is usual for evaluation procedures to start with a compliance check. Its purpose is to verify whether the proposal conforms with the client's requirements for information and presents a complete response to the work specification. The questions that the compliance check asks include:

- Did the proposal arrive on time? If it was late, will you accept it? This will normally depend on the criticality of the deadline, the degree of lateness and the reason for delay. There are circumstances in which applying a strict and consistent deadline may save you from complaints of bias and unfairness.

- Does the proposal contain all the information requested?

- Do the consultants say they will fulfil all your requirements or are there some they say they cannot meet?

- Is information set out in the required form – for example, using a template that you may have supplied so as to obtain a consistent presentation?

- Does the approach put forward in the proposal conform fully with the work specification or are there differences? Are the consultants proposing a 'variant solution'?

- If formal statements are required, for example on environmental, industrial relations or health and safety policies or on the avoidance of conflicts of interest, are they included?

- If consultants have been asked to submit other statements in their proposals – for example insurance certificates, letters of commitment from personnel or members of a consortium or declarations about the extent of subcontracting – are they present?

If there are information requirements you regard as critical, include them in a compliance check. But take care not to confuse issues of compliance with the points on which the relative merits of proposals are assessed. It would be a mistake, for example, to decide that only proposals showing good value for money were compliant and thus eligible for evaluation, since the identification of good value for money is usually one of the outcomes of an evaluation.

Checking for compliance may seem a rather bureaucratic procedure but it does serve a useful purpose. Bidders are assumed to be competent enough to realize that, when a client asks for certain information or requests that it is presented in a certain way, the client has a reason for doing so. Consultants who ignore your instructions or fail to grasp what you want from them, and who put the proposal together in a way that suits them rather than you, are also likely to be inattentive to your requirements when it comes to performing the work.

Where information is missing, incomplete or set out in an incorrect format, you have a choice of either rejecting the proposal or giving the consultants an opportunity to put matters right. Be guided by the seriousness of the error or omission and by common sense. Even though you may have given consultants ample time to prepare a proposal and supplied them with templates, they can still get things wrong. This is particularly the case when it comes to setting out cost estimates, perhaps because their accounts people find that the way they structure this information is hard to adapt to the requirements of individual clients.

Unless you want to take a hard line, send the consultants an e-mail or fax to warn of impending rejection and allow them a little time to remedy the deficiency. It is surprising how on these occasions consultants can manage to do in an hour what they had failed to achieve in a month! The important point is to be fair and reasonable. This initial check will also tell you if any proposal is a non-starter, for example where the consultants do not have the required qualifications. You cannot afford to waste time and money evaluating proposals that have no chance of succeeding.

Occasionally, you can see at a glance that the consultants have entirely misunderstood the purpose of a proposal. Instead of a practical business offer that focuses on your needs and directly addresses your requirements, they have given you what amounts to a self-centred marketing document filled with platitudes about their breadth of capabilities and range of services. You will find little in its pages that is specific to your business situation. The emphasis is on 'what we do' and 'what we offer' rather than 'what you want from us'. If that is the tone of the document, you might question whether it is worth considering further.

Evaluating proposals

It is then time to analyse in detail the proposals that do appear to offer a serious response. Arriving at a decision may be a matter of simply grading each proposal as a whole, rather like entries in many other types of competition. For example, a proposal that failed to meet any of your key requirements might be given zero points, while one that met them all might receive, say, five points. Each proposal's score would reflect the extent to which it matched your preferences overall.

But in many instances a more analytical method will be necessary, one that allows you to assess the relative and differing merits of each proposal. For instance:

- Proposal A may offer the most convincing technical solution but quote the highest level of costs.

- Proposal B may have a price that fits more comfortably within your budget but the CVs of the people named as doing the work may be unimpressive and not all the information you asked for may be present.

- Proposal C may be middle-of-the-road in terms of price and technical response but put forward good ideas that no other competitor had thought of.

How do you choose between them? The answer is to adopt a structured and consistent method of evaluation based on a defined set of criteria, as outlined here.

For most businesses as well as clients in the public sector, value for money is the prime consideration influencing the selection of consultants. Value for money is not necessarily identical with the lowest price, as any shopper will know. It reflects a balance between price, performance and quality. A low price can be seductive but it can also tempt you into false economies. It is best practice not to award a contract on price alone but to view price as part of a value-for-money assessment. The fees you pay to consultants will often be just a fraction of the total costs of achieving your business objectives, yet the cost-effectiveness and sustainability of your plans may depend critically on the quality of the advice obtained from them. And the fees you pay have to be a reasonable reward for the services provided and the work performed. This is why it is so important to develop a realistic estimate of costs as part of the work specification (Chapter 4).

Draw up a list of criteria, the factors you will use to judge the proposals (Figure 5.14). Price will be there, perhaps heading the list, but you should also include the practicality of the proposed work plan, the skills and experience of the people who would do the work, the degree to which the proposal shows an understanding of your requirements, and the general quality of the proposal. If consultants are working for you at present or have undertaken contracts for you in the past, their performance record will be a key criterion in judging the credibility of their proposals. You will want to take account, for example, of their quality of service, their adherence to cost and time estimates and the extent to which you and they have developed a satisfactory working relationship.

In developing an example here, let's assume that there is no past performance to consider. Apply the five criteria noted above – price, work plan, skills and experience, understanding of requirements and quality of the proposal. To make the process objective, adopt a marking scheme based on these criteria. The marking scheme needs to recognize that some criteria are more important to you than others, and so they need to have more weight in the calculation.

If price is the most important criterion, you might attach to it 30 per cent of the possible marks. The work plan might have 25 per cent, and the other three criteria – people's skills and experience, the consultants' understanding of your requirements and the quality of the proposal – might each have 15 per cent. Score each proposal against each of the five criteria on a scale of 0 to 10. Then multiply each score out of 10 by the relevant weighting factor, add up the multiplied scores and divide by 10 to obtain the proposal's total score out of 100.

Does this sound complicated? Well, Figure 5.15 shows how the calculation works. Remember that you are looking only at one example: the actual criteria you apply and the weightings you give to them should depend in each case on the specific nature of the work. In addition to the criteria used in the example, there may be other important points to take account of, such as the consultants' performance record on comparable work (including work for other clients), the reliability of their expertise, their management ability and their capacity to deliver an innovative and imaginative response to problems. All of these have a part to play in helping you select the consultants best suited to undertake the work.

Alternatively, you might adopt the procedure followed by consumer magazines when testing products. Rate the proposals against qualitative criteria, ignoring price, to identify the proposal offering the closest

Compliance

- Have the consultants provided all the information you asked for?
- Have they confirmed that they can do everything you want?

Price

- Is their total price stated clearly?
- Does it come within your budget?
- Can you tell how their price was arrived at?
- Is it realistic?
- Does it offer good value for money?
- If it is unusually low, do you need to find out why?

Work plan

- Does it meet your requirements?
- Does it match your assessment of the effort and resources needed?
- Does it look sensible and cost-effective?
- Has it been thought through in detail?
- Will it hit your targets and deadlines?
- Have the consultants justified any proposed variations from your work specification?
- Do they propose to subcontract any of the work?

Competence and experience

- Have they given facts and figures about their work record?
- Can they provide the necessary skills to do the work properly?
- Are the people who will be doing the work named?
- Are they appropriately qualified?

Performance and management

- Does the proposal show a conscientious approach to managing the work?
- Does it pay due attention to quality, efficient performance and prompt delivery?
- Have the consultants thought ahead to the problems that might occur and proposed ways of managing risks?
- Does the proposal convince you that the working relationship will be successful?

Quality and proposal

- Is it a well organized and competently produced document?
- Does it accurately reflect the work specification?
- Does it show insight and an ability to get to the heart of issues?
- Does it offer added value in a way that sets it apart from other proposals?
- Have the consultants made it easy to find the information you need?
- Is the proposal uncertain or evasive on any point?

Figure 5.14 _Summary of evaluation criteria_

1. Establish the percentage weighting of criteria.

Price	30
Work plan	25
Skills and experience	15
Understanding of requirements	15
Quality of proposal	15

2. Score the proposals out of 10 on each criterion.

	Proposal A	Proposal B	Proposal C
Price	7	7	8
Work plan	7	6	6
Skills and experience	7	8	6
Understanding of requirements	8	6	7
Quality of proposal	8	6	6

3. Multiply scores by weighting factors, add the scores and divide by 10.

	Proposal A	Proposal B	Proposal C
Price	210	210	240
Work plan	175	150	150
Skills and experience	105	120	90
Understanding of requirements	120	90	105
Quality of proposal	120	90	90
TOTAL	730	660	675
Score out of 100	**73.0**	**66.0**	**67.5**

The relative weakness of the team named in Proposal C and deficiencies in the presentation of this proposal counteracted its price advantage. Proposal B put forward a more competent team than Proposal C, but showed less insight into the client's requirements. Proposal A was a clear winner – a well-prepared and presented proposal offering the best all-round value with an acceptable price and a good understanding of the client's intentions.

Figure 5.15 *Example of a proposal marking scheme*

match to your work specification. Then bring price into the calculation to decide which proposal is your 'best buy'. If the one with most technical merit is no more expensive than its competitors, you have a clear winner. But you might be willing to trade off some technical shortcomings against a lower price and decide that on balance a different proposal offers the best value for money.

Here are questions to ask as you are going through the evaluation.

Price

- Is there a clear statement of the total estimated price and how it was arrived at?

- Are tables and cost schedules arithmetically correct?

- If price information is set out in several tables, are the sums consistent?

- Have any cost items been accounted for more than once or omitted?

- Is the price realistic and within your budget? Is there a convincing match between the price quoted and the scale and quality of the services offered?

- Does the price include items that were not asked for in your requirements? Do they strengthen or weaken the value for money of the proposal?

- Have the consultants applied a contingency margin across the board, even to items of work that carry no exceptional risk?

- Are there unexplained items in the schedules, such as 'other administrative costs'? Do you need to find out what these are?

- Is it clear how costs were calculated?

- If the price seems unusually low, do you need to check out why? There are several possible reasons that may account for it:

  - Perhaps the consultants did not understand your requirements or the technical demands of the work.

  - They may have miscalculated their costs or failed to match the financial and technical aspects of their bid.

  - They may have underpriced their bid as a competitive ploy. They may hope to recoup the costs on other, fixed price jobs that take less time than was budgeted for. Or perhaps their order book is a bit thin and they need the job in order to keep staff busy on chargeable work. If the contract is time-based (Chapter 6) they may be relying on cost overruns to make the work viable; if it is a fixed price contract, they may hope to be able to negotiate additional fees through overpriced contract modifications.

   – On the other hand, they may have ways of doing things that allow them to cut costs while still delivering reliable results.

■ The best advice is to treat an abnormally low price as an amber light that may signal a high level of risk. Don't reject the bid out of hand; give the consultants a chance to explain and justify their price.

Work plan

■ Does the work plan look sensible and cost-effective? Does it show a realistic input of time and resources?

■ Has it been thought through in detail and communicated effectively, or does it need further explanation?

■ Is there a clear statement of exactly what the consultants will deliver as outcomes of the work, and when?

■ If the work is priced on a time charge basis, does the work plan include time spent 'mobilizing' a team, and does that seem reasonable? The costs may be justifiable when a team and its equipment have to be assembled in a logistically complicated situation, but mobilization costs are sometimes used as a device to recoup part of the expense of bidding for the work.

■ If you have stressed that hitting targets and deadlines will be critical, has this been recognized in the proposal?

■ How close a match is there between the work plan and management arrangements in the proposal and your own assessment of the practical demands of the work?

■ If the proposal puts forward an alternative approach or a variant solution, does it make a good case for this?

■ Do the consultants say they intend to subcontract any part of the work? If so, how much and why?

VIEWPOINT

'Our divisional managers use their commercial judgement in appointing consultants and other advisers. When they take these decisions they have a lot at stake professionally. Their futures in the group can depend on the way their contracts work out. No one wants to be seen as a manager who lets contracts run out of control. So we look for consultants who understand the way we work and the importance we attach to efficient delivery. The worst thing consultants can do is to fill their bids with nice words and brave promises but then fail to deliver. It's bad for us and for them – we won't use them any more.'

(Chief executive of a banking and financial services group)

Business approach

- Have the consultants recognized your business objectives and priorities?

- Do they seem to understand the way your business environment works?

- Do they offer benefits that can improve your organization's performance and competitiveness? Would the fees paid to them give a good return on investment?

- Does the proposal have a businesslike feel? If you have asked for innovation, is it there?

- Does it convince you that the consultants have done the job successfully before?

- Does it give you a sense of synergy and business compatibility?

Competence and experience

- Are claims about the consultants' achievements and record backed up by facts and evidence, for example by details of similar contracts?

- Is their experience recent and relevant to the work you have in mind?

- Is there any indication of whether the experience you are reading about was gained by the people who would be working for you?

- How well qualified are the people named in the proposal? Do they have the necessary competence and expertise?

- What is their employment status with the consultants?

- If the consultants are putting forward a team, what is the added value of each individual? Are there people in the team who do not seem to have a defined technical function? In particular, does their team look overloaded at a senior management level – ie with individuals who cost a lot but do not seem to be contributing anything specific?

- Have the consultants included CVs of key subcontractor personnel?

Can you believe all you read in CVs?

The CV that appears in a consultancy proposal is (or ought to be) different from the sort of CV that accompanies a job application. Instead of focusing on career objectives, capabilities and the capacity to take on new responsibilities, it should display the person's experience, background and value as a resource of expertise, and the results and benefits that he or she has achieved for clients. These credentials should be backed up by facts and figures – assignments undertaken, responsibilities fulfilled, contract values and so forth.

As you read a CV, ask:

- Is there solid evidence of successful work for other clients and successful achievement as a team member?

- Does the person possess the competencies you have in mind for the work?

- Looking at the person's age and experience, does what he or she has achieved match his or her qualifications, or are the qualifications more impressive than the achievements?

One rarely comes across a CV that is grossly distorted by lies, though people do sometimes misrepresent their competencies.

For instance, they may put forward an image of themselves as consultants on the basis of their technical knowledge, whereas in reality they may lack the ability to interact with clients in a constructive working relationship.

People often put a favourable slant on their experience – for example, claiming greater responsibility than they actually had or glossing over details that might not portray them in the most helpful light (does the word 'spin' spring to mind?). Watch out for the high-risk 'experts' – people who roam nomadically from one sector of consultancy to another, without any clear pattern of professional commitment.

The best course is to read the CV carefully and try to form an overall picture of the person's suitability. Does everything add up? Is the record of experience convincing? Would this person be useful in meeting your objectives? And does he or she look better on paper than the people named in other proposals?

Performance and management

- How have the consultants dealt with responsibilities for the management and direction of the work? Is there a clear and direct line of accountability?

- If you have emphasized the need for performance monitoring and progress measurement, have they responded convincingly?

- Have they recognized the importance of taking action to forestall problems?

- Is there an appropriate focus on quality management and output delivery?

Quality of the proposal

- Does the proposal give an impression of professionalism and reliability?

- Does it offer a distinctive added value that makes it different from other proposals?

- Does it focus on the points you consider important?

- Are there ideas in the proposal that are so good, you wish you had thought of them yourself?

- Does the proposal appear to have been written expressly for you, to match your requirements, or has it been assembled by copy-and-paste methods?

- Are there signs of genuine commitment and involvement, or does the proposal seem a routine exercise?

- Have the consultants simply fed back the information you supplied and dressed it up to give the appearance that it is their own work, or has the information been applied in ways that show insight and perception and tell you something new? If they have simply repeated word for word what you told them, perhaps they had nothing of their own to say or perhaps they were afraid of saying the wrong thing.

- Are the messages in the proposal consistent with what you were told at meetings?

- Is the proposal well organized? Is it easy to locate the information you are looking for? If consultants are helpful in making information accessible as well as successfully competitive in their technical response, they are likely to prove effective professional colleagues.

- Constructing sentences that actually make sense and are free from errors of grammar and spelling is probably not the field of expertise for which you are engaging consultants; but poor communication on their part will be a drawback if the work requires them to produce coherent and effective reports and other documents. If their proposals (which after all are meant to impress you) are carelessly prepared, how can you trust them to do a competent job?

- If the consultants were giving a verbal presentation and chose to address you in a breathless gabble, you would quickly become irritated, switch off and wish you were somewhere else. Badly presented tables, with information crammed into rows and columns in a diminutive font size, have pretty much the same effect. The consultants have not thought about your need to receive information in a form that is easily readable – a discouraging sign.

Before finalizing your decision, you may want consultants to follow up their proposals with presentations or interviews where they can answer questions that have emerged from your analysis of their responses and expand on points made in their proposals. After a preferred consultant has been identified, there may be a need to negotiate the terms of the offer to get a better deal and better value for money. Negotiations with consultants are discussed in Chapter 6.

When you have decided on the consultants you want to use, ask them to confirm in writing that they are ready to undertake the work. Once the contract for the work is signed (not before!), write to the consultants who were unsuccessful to thank them for their interest and perhaps explain why you were unable to accept their bid.

Case Study

The subject of the tender was the supply of freight-forwarding services for an oil and gas development project. Its scope covered pre-planning, management and other activities required for the movement of project equipment and materials by road, rail, ship and air to the project location. The budget available to the client was £830,000.

The objective of the tendering process was to identify the contractor most likely to provide the services in an efficient, timely and cost-effective manner and to deliver best value to the project. Five firms were invited to tender, selected from the client's supplier database on the basis of their capability, past performance and experience in project freight forwarding within the UK and Europe.

The tender evaluation had two main parts: technical and commercial. The technical evaluation was concerned with five elements:

- the contractor's method statement, which was required to show a perceptive understanding of the logistical complexities of the work;

- the experience and quality of the contractor's nominated management staff;

- the contractor's present and forecast workload and other commitments during the contract period;

- the proposed reimbursement method for the services;

- the contractor's quality assurance and quality control programme.

The commercial evaluation was structured to reflect quantified movements of freight (lump sum elements) and model cases related to UK and European volumetric/distance rates so as to obtain a means of comparing the contractors like for like and identifying price loading.

In the technical evaluation, the contractors' responses on each of the five elements were scored from 1 (unsatisfactory with many weaknesses; able to undertake the services but unlikely to meet the desired standards of performance) to 5 (outstanding; expected to exceed significantly the desired standards of performance). Following an initial assessment, the two highest-scoring responses underwent a detailed technical examination. This identified a clear technical front runner, though minor aspects of the tender needed to be clarified before a contract could be awarded.

The commercial evaluation showed that this same contractor was the only one among the five tenderers to submit a price within the client's budget and to make no qualifications in its tender. The others had priced their bids from 35 to almost 50 per cent above the budget figure.

The evaluation team recommended that the contract should be awarded to this contractor subject to the outstanding technical points being resolved. The contractor was called to a clarification meeting where the items were discussed and agreed, after which the contract was signed.

If you are not satisfied with any of the proposals, you will have to start again. This may mean seeking proposals from a different set of consultants or inviting new bids from those you approached previously. But before embarking on another round, find time to analyse the reasons why you were dissatisfied with the proposals and look critically at your handling of the tendering process.

Perhaps the way you expressed your requirements or the timetable you set made it difficult for consultants to make an effective bid. Put things right before going out to tender again. If you decide to approach the same consultants, explain to them how you have changed the process or revised the work specification so as to achieve a better result. Having once invested time and money at your request in a bid that got nowhere, they will need to be convinced that they have a greater chance of success this time.

What to look for when choosing consultants

- A real identification with your needs and objectives.

- An understanding of how your business operates.

- An ability to provide much more than basic analysis.

- A sense of genuine commitment and dependability.

- A clear statement of who will do the work, how it will be done, what results will be delivered and when.

- A convincing indication of value for money and quality performance.

- Recommendations from other clients – plus a strong record of comparable experience.

- A positive approach to collaborating with your staff.

- Added value for your business through the transfer of skills and reinforcement of competencies.

Dear Sir

This letter sets out the basis on which we are to act as your tax agent and tax adviser.

Your spouse is legally responsible for her own tax affairs and will be dealt with independently, if required. If at any time you require us to consider your joint tax or financial affairs, it will be necessary to agree the scope of our work in writing with both spouses.

1. Our service to you

1.1 We will prepare annual accounts for your consideration and approval from the books, records, vouchers and other information produced to us. The accounts shall be in the form of income and expenditure accounts prepared according to generally accepted accounting principles. Whilst we shall examine the records and make such inquiries as we consider necessary to enable us to prepare these accounts, we shall not carry out an audit in the sense required by statute for companies. The first year for which we will prepare the accounts falls into the tax year ended 5 April 2003.

The accounts will contain a declaration, for your signature, that you approve the accounts and have made available all relevant records and information for their preparation.

Figure 5.16 _Example of a letter of agreement from a firm of accountants_

We shall report with such variations as we consider necessary that we have prepared, without carrying out an audit, the accounts from the

accounting records presented to us and from the information and explanations given to us.

1.2 We will prepare your personal tax return together with such supporting schedules as are appropriate and will calculate your liability for tax and national insurance contributions.

1.3 We will send you your tax return and supporting schedules for you to approve and sign. We will then submit it to the Inland Revenue. You authorize us to file the return electronically. The first return that we shall be responsible for preparing will be that for the year ended 5 April 2003.

1.4 We will tell you how much tax and national insurance contributions you should pay and when. If appropriate we will initiate repayment claims when tax has been overpaid. We will advise you as to suitable payments on account and the due dates for payment. As your agent we are authorized to claim for reduced payments on account based on any information you have supplied to us. However, you are responsible for ensuring that we are kept informed of all material changes to your tax affairs as they arise.

1.5 We will deal with the Inland Revenue regarding any amendments required to your return and prepare any amended returns that may be required.

1.6 We will advise as to possible claims and elections arising from the tax return and from information supplied by you. Where instructed by you, we will make such claims and elections in the form and manner required by the Inland Revenue.

1.7 We will submit form 64-8 as signed by you to the Inland Revenue. This form authorizes the Inland Revenue to correspond with us on your behalf and to send us copies of formal notices. However, this authority does not apply to all Inland Revenue correspondence and you should therefore always send us the originals or copies of communications you receive from them.

1.8 If the Inland Revenue chooses your return for inquiry, this work may need to be the subject of a separate assignment in which case we will seek further instructions from you.

1.9 We shall be pleased to advise you on matters relating to tax and general financial planning. This may include advice in connection with specific

Figure 5.16 *continued*

transactions, or advice in relation to the tax-efficient organization of your financial affairs. We are also able to advise in relation to corporation tax, value added tax, trustee and executorship work and capital taxes planning. To enable us to do this you will need to instruct us in good time. Because tax rules change frequently you must ask us to review any advice already given if a transaction is delayed, or if an apparently similar transaction is to be undertaken. It is our policy to confirm in writing advice upon which you may wish to rely.

2. Your responsibilities: provision of information by you

2.1 You are legally responsible for making correct returns by the due date and for payment of tax on time. Failure to meet the deadlines may result in automatic penalties, surcharges and/or interest.

2.2 To enable us to carry out our work you agree:

2.2.1 that all returns are to be made on the basis of full disclosure of all sources of income, charges, allowances and capital transactions;

2.2.2 to provide full information necessary for dealing with your affairs: we will rely on the information and documents being true, correct and complete and will not audit the information or those documents;

2.2.3 that we can approach such third parties as may be appropriate for information that we consider necessary to deal with your affairs;

2.2.4 to provide us with information in sufficient time for your tax return to be completed and submitted by the due date following the end of the tax year. We will use our reasonable endeavours to complete the return on time but, if the information is not provided by 30 November and, as a result, the preparation and submission of the return is delayed, interest, penalties and/or surcharges may arise for which you will be responsible;

2.2.5 to forward to us on receipt copies of all Inland Revenue communications and correspondence to enable us to deal with them as may be necessary within the statutory time limits;

2.2.6 to keep us informed about significant changes in your circumstances if they are likely to affect your tax position; and

2.2.7 to keep and retain records and financial information in support of your annual tax returns for certain statutory periods of up to five years from the filing date (31 January after the end of the tax year) as required by the Taxes Acts. The period may be extended if the Inland Revenue

Figure 5.16 _continued_

inquires into your tax return. Failure to retain such records can result in penalties being sought by the Revenue.

2.3 We will provide our professional services outlined in this letter with reasonable care and skill. However, we will not be responsible for any losses, penalties, surcharges, interest or additional tax liabilities arising from the supply by you or others of incorrect or incomplete information, or your or others' failure to supply any appropriate information or your failure to act on our advice or respond promptly to communications from us or the tax authorities.

3. Ethical and practice guidelines

3.1 We shall observe the by-laws, regulations and ethical guidelines of the Institute of Chartered Accountants in England and Wales and accept instructions to act for you on the basis that we will act in accordance with those guidelines. A copy of these guidelines is available for your inspection in our offices.

3.2 *You authorize us to advise the Inland Revenue of any errors that it may make in dealing with your tax affairs (other than where the tax at stake is* de minimis*) to enable us to comply with our professional responsibilities and to correct its errors as appropriate, having first obtained your approval.*

3.3 We may use either our own employees or persons seconded to us by third parties when performing our obligations under the terms of this agreement.

4. Indemnity

4.1 We will accept liability for our fraud, negligence or wilful default or material breach by us of a term of this agreement and you will indemnify and hold us harmless and indemnify our affiliated partnerships and companies and our and their respective partners, directors, officers, employees, agents and professional advisers (together 'indemnified persons') and hold them harmless from and against all other losses, claims, actions, proceedings, demands, damages, liabilities, costs and expenses (together 'losses') arising out of or in connection with this agreement other than any losses caused by an indemnified person's fraud, negligence or wilful default.

4.2 Our liability shall be limited to that proportion of any loss or damage (including interest and costs) that is ascribed to us by a court of competent jurisdiction or arbitrator allocating proportionate responsibility to us having regard to the contributions to the loss or damage in question

Figure 5.16 *continued*

by any person (loss and damage having the same meaning as in the Civil Liability (Contribution) Act 1978).

4.3 No claim in respect of this agreement shall be brought personally against any individuals involved in the performance of the services under this agreement, whether actual or deemed parties or employees, agents or professional advisers.

4.4 The advice that we give to you is for your sole use and does not constitute advice to any third party to whom you may communicate it. We accept no responsibility to third parties for any aspect of our professional services or work that is made available to them.

4.5 The provisions of this paragraph shall remain in full force and effect after the termination of this agreement.

5. Confidentiality

5.1 We confirm that where you give us confidential information we shall, at all times, keep it confidential, except as required by law or as provided for in regulatory, ethical or other professional requirements applicable to us.

5.2 You agree that it will be sufficient compliance with our duty of confidence for us to take such steps as we in good faith think fit to preserve confidential information both during and after termination of this engagement.

5.3 Neither we nor any of our employees or agents shall have any duty to disclose to you any information that comes to our or their attention in the course of carrying on any other business or as a result of or in connection with the provision of services to other persons.

6. Electronic communication

6.1 We may communicate with you by e-mail. Although electronic transmission of information cannot be guaranteed to be secure or virus or error free, we will use reasonable procedures to ensure that they are. It is your responsibility to carry out a virus check on any attachments received.

6.2 As Internet communications are capable of data corruption we do not accept any responsibility for changes made to such communications after their despatch. All risks connected with sending commercially sensitive information relating to your business are borne by you and are not our responsibility. If you do not accept this risk, you should notify us in writing that e-mail is not an acceptable means of communication.

Figure 5.16 _continued_

7. Retention of documents

7.1 Whilst certain documents may legally belong to you, we intend to destroy correspondence and other papers that we store that are more than 10 years old, other than documents that we consider to be of continuing significance. If you require retention of any documents you must indicate that fact to us.

8. Fees

8.1 Our fees are based upon the degree of responsibility and skill involved and the time necessarily occupied on the work. It is our practice to render fees regularly on the basis of costs incurred.

8.2 Fees are due upon presentation. We may terminate our engagement and cease acting if payment of any fees is unduly delayed. However, it is not our intention to use these arrangements in a way that is unfair or unreasonable.

9. Client monies

9.1 We may, from time to time, hold money on your behalf. Such money will be held in trust in a client bank account, which is segregated from the company's funds.

10. Data protection

10.1 We are required to comply with the provisions of the Data Protection Act 1998 in relation to the processing of any personal data we obtain from you. We may process all the details we obtain from you to enable us to advise you in accordance with the terms of this letter. We may also request with your consent further information from third parties such as your previous accountant.

10.2 Any information gathered will only be used for the purpose set out in this letter.

10.3 We may disclose your personal data as required by law, to the Inland Revenue, for example, or to any third parties who process personal data on our behalf. You have a right of access, under data protection legislation, to the personal data that we hold about you.

11. Applicable law

11.1 This engagement letter shall be governed by, and construed in accordance with, English law. The Courts of England shall have

Figure 5.16 *continued*

exclusive jurisdiction in relation to any claim, dispute or difference concerning the engagement letter and any matter arising from it. Each party irrevocably waives any right they may have to object to an action being brought in those Courts, to claim that the action has been brought in an inappropriate forum, or to claim that those Courts do not have jurisdiction.

11.2 A person who is not an express party to this agreement shall have no right under the Contracts (Rights of Third Parties) Act 1999 to enforce any terms of this agreement or to consent to any purported amendment to the terms of this agreement, but this does not affect any right or remedy of a third party that exists or is available other than under the provisions of that Act.

11.3 Notwithstanding paragraph 11.2, any person indemnified under paragraph 4 may enforce the terms of paragraph 5 subject to and in accordance with the provisions of the Contracts (Rights of Third Parties) Act 1999.

12. Assignment or novation

12.1 Neither party may assign any of their respective rights under this agreement to any third party without written consent. However, we may transfer all rights, duties and obligations under this agreement to any successor in the conduct of our business. In the event that such a successor, be it a partnership, a limited liability partnership or a body corporate, takes over the business then you agree that all the obligations under this agreement may be provided by the successor and that this letter and your agreement to this letter will constitute written agreement to the future novation of this contract in favour of the successor entity.

13. Help us to give you the best service

13.1 If at any time you would like to discuss with us how our service to you could be improved or if you are dissatisfied with the service you are receiving, please let us know by contacting .... who is the relevant departmental compliance officer.

13.2 We undertake to look into any complaint carefully and promptly and to do all we can to explain the position to you. If we do not answer your complaint to your satisfaction, you may of course take up the matter with the Institute. In the unlikely event that we cannot meet our liabilities to you, you may be able to claim compensation under the Chartered Accountants' Compensation Scheme.

Figure 5.16 _continued_

14. Agreement of terms

14.1 This letter supersedes any previous engagement letter for the period covered. Once agreed, this letter will remain effective from the date of signature until it is replaced. You or we may terminate our authority to act on your behalf at any time without penalty. Notice of termination must be given in writing. All accrued unpaid fees and disbursements will be payable immediately after the termination of this agreement.

14.2 Please confirm your agreement to the terms of this letter by signing and returning the enclosed copy.

14.3 If this letter is not in accordance with your understanding of the scope of our engagement, please let us know.

Yours faithfully for and on behalf of ....

I acknowledge receipt of this letter, which fully records the agreement between us relating to your appointment to carry out the work described in it.

Signature of Client: ....

Date: ....

Figure 5.16 *continued*

6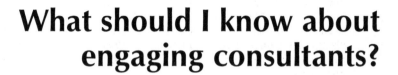

What should I know about engaging consultants?

AGREEMENTS AND CONTRACTS

In law a contractual relationship does not depend on having a written agreement: it is not unknown for a consultant to finish a piece of work before the client gets round to drawing up a contract for it. But that leaves the door wide open for misunderstanding and exposes both the client and the consultant to an unacceptable level of risk. The best advice is to have a contract or a letter of engagement in place before the work starts, and to agree this document as soon as practicable after deciding on your choice of consultant. Do not rely just on a conversation or an assumption that the consultant knows what you want – put things in writing!

As noted in Chapter 5, consultants may produce standard forms of contract or terms of engagement that their professional institutions or trade associations require or advise them to use (Figures 5.4 and 5.6). These are documents applicable to almost all types of consultancy or advisory work undertaken by members, and the contractual terms will be fair and equitable provided that the organization is a reputable body. You will need to have convincing reasons if you want your consultants to depart from them. Still, check through the document to make sure there is nothing that causes you concern. If you don't fully understand any point, ask the consultants to explain it: if even then you are uncertain, seek legal advice.

You may sometimes be asked to sign an agreement of the consultants' own invention. In that case it is essential to read every clause carefully – particularly the small print! Don't assume the consultants must have your best interests at heart. Make sure you know exactly what you are committing yourself to as a client. Points to watch out for include the following requirements:

- that an advance payment is to be made to the consultants, for example on signature of the contract or agreement, or to meet specific expenses such as local authority fees or the cost of instructing counsel;

- that invoices are to be paid within a time span defined by the consultants, failing which interest is to be charged at a rate defined by the consultants;

- that the consultants are to be indemnified for any claims, damages or costs incurred through their infringements of intellectual property rights;

- that estimates of time and cost for completing the work are to be regarded as informal calculations liable to adjustment and review as necessary;

- that the consultants have the right to assign or subcontract parts of the work to professional associates or outside staff because of time constraints or on grounds of efficiency;

- that the maximum liability of the consultants is to be limited to the amount paid for the work;

- that the consultants will rely on the client's disclosure of the facts of a situation and that the agreement does not represent a commitment to obtain a particular outcome;

- that the agreement will be renewed automatically for a further term, typically one year, if the contract is not terminated within a specified period of notice prior to the end of the current term – this is sometimes called an 'evergreen clause';

■ that nothing in the contract documents is to modify or affect the standard conditions set out in the agreement.

So far as late payment is concerned, UK legislation (The Late Payment of Commercial Debts (Interest) Act 1998) allows a business, whatever its size, to claim interest on an account outstanding for more than 30 days, provided that the customer has been made aware of its payment terms before work is contracted. The rate of interest is calculated as the Bank of England base rate at the end of the last day of the 30-day term plus 8 per cent. The principle of charging interest for late payment is reasonable, since the consultants will probably not be in a position to extend credit facilities to a client; but you need to check the rate of interest proposed.

Other requirements listed above reflect an attempt on the part of the consultants to transfer to the client as much as possible of the risk inherent in a consultancy assignment. The extent to which these requirements seem fair and reasonable is a matter for you to judge, taking into account the context of the work. What you are being asked to sign up to is probably not what you would have agreed had you and the consultants jointly developed a contract in which risks were allocated rather then transferred. You will need to be convinced that the terms the consultants want you to accept make business sense in terms of overall costs and benefits. Will you gain better value from taking a risk yourself than from paying the consultants to take it for you? Bear in mind also that in law the implicit duty of care and diligence noted below can override any restrictive conditions that consultants may seek to include in a contract or agreement.

If there are points you are uncomfortable with in the agreement, question them. If there are clauses you cannot agree to, cross them out. Sign an agreement only if you can accept it in full.

Large businesses and other corporate organizations normally have their own standard terms of contract. If you are a non-profit organization or belong to a trade association or interest group, you may find that there are standard or sample consultancy agreements available for you to use.

But it will often be left to you to produce a contract document. If the work is straightforward and you have experience of engaging consultants, you should be able to prepare an agreement at least in draft without having to seek legal advice – though in a corporate environment you may need to consult the procurement arm of your organization or a legal services unit. In most instances, the contract can quite adequately take the form of a letter or a series of paragraphs under headings, as long as all the necessary points are covered and everything is stated unambiguously and in a way that correctly expresses your intentions. Formal documents laced with 'whereas' and 'hereinafter' should be strictly for large-scale assignments.

Even so, it would be a false economy not to pay the cost of one hour or so of a lawyer's time to have your draft checked through. If you are unsure about the best way to phrase a point, or if the work carries a significant level of financial or professional risk, don't attempt a DIY approach – use a lawyer to help draw up the agreement.

A contract has been described as a meeting of minds. Both parties must understand correctly its content, its intention and their respective responsibilities and liabilities. Whatever the specific context, the relationship between the two parties will be subject to the general law of contract. In any contract or agreement for services, several points are implicit:

- that there is an offer, an acceptance and a mutual exchange of benefits;

- that both parties will do their best to perform the contract successfully;

- that the consultant will exercise reasonable care and diligence in undertaking the work;

- that the results of the work will be given to the client within a reasonable time – unless specific times are expressly agreed;

- that the consultant will be paid a sum that is a reasonable remuneration for his or her services – unless a specific fee is expressly agreed.

Contracts can look intimidating, with their apparent emphasis on dissatisfaction, disputes and termination. If contracts are supposed to be meetings of minds, you may ask, why are these topics given such prominence? They are in the contract not because there is an expectation of disappointment and conflict, but to define an agreed course of action that can resolve matters as painlessly as possible should problems arise. The more thoughtfully a contract is drafted, the less likely the work is to run into difficulties.

The two most damaging faults in contracts are uncertainty and rigidity. Perhaps the key thing that a contract does is to assign risks between the parties – principally the risk that costs will turn out significantly more than was estimated. It is essential that the way the contract is worded makes its meaning on this point absolutely clear and proof against misunderstanding. Vagueness in the terms of a contract will lead to friction, with irreparable consequences for the success of the work.

But it is important not to go to the other extreme by spelling out every requirement in the most minute detail or making the terms of the contract inflexible. Clients who pin consultants down about the precise methods and procedures to be followed look as if they are saying 'We don't trust you to do things right', which is likely to provoke a corresponding response from consultants. Similarly, as noted in Chapter 4, a large-scale or long-term project is bound to encounter conditions that call for adjustments in the scope of the work or require a change of approach. The best strategy is to plan for these contingencies when developing the work specification.

VIEWPOINT

'I have worked a lot with consultants and have seen a lot of money wasted. Not because they were slack or incompetent, but because the client – my bosses – hadn't planned or managed the contract effectively, hadn't understood what shape the final output would take and hadn't provided the resources to put results into action. It is easy to blame consultants if they deliver their work late, but in my experience it is clients who are the biggest sinners when it comes to missing targets and deadlines.

'Another problem is that clients often short-change themselves by not being prepared to pay for value. Their accountants can have a narrow, short-term perspective: sometimes they seem more content to make false economies than to buy real value. People use 'return on investment' as a catchphrase, but actually that's a useful way of looking at the consultancy transaction. If you view consultancy as an investment instead of an expense, you can see that you have to put thought and effort into getting the specification right, getting the contract right and helping the relationship to deliver a good return.'

(Business manager, Internet services provider)

TYPES OF CONTRACT

The type of contract you adopt for a particular piece of work needs to be right for that work if the outcome is to be successful, which means it has to reflect the level of risk and uncertainty attached to the performance of the contract. So far as contracts for consultancy services are concerned, there are three principal options, which are related largely to the fee bases outlined in Chapter 3:

■ a fixed price contract: this is sometimes, not altogether correctly, referred to as a 'lump sum' contract – the term 'lump sum' implies a single payment, whereas payments on fixed price contracts are often made in instalments as tasks or stages of the work programme are completed;

■ a time-based contract, sometimes called a cost-plus contract, ie the cost of the work plus the multiplier applied by the consultant and the agreed expenses;

■ a call-off or term contract.

In a **fixed price contract** the work or services are provided for a price agreed between you and the consultants and written into the contract, as in Figure 6.1. The price may be the sum quoted by the consultants in their proposal, or a sum predetermined by you on the basis of the work specification, or a price that has to lie within a defined limit or below a budget ceiling. The essence of the contract is that the price you pay can change only if the contract is changed. Bear in mind that Figure 6.1 and the other contracts and letters of engagement reproduced in the chapter are shown only as examples of contractual style and content. As noted in the Preface, they are not intended as models or templates, and it would be rash to copy them verbatim for one's own use.

A fixed price contract will limit your financial liability, and that may be its main attraction; but at the same time you may limit the quality and usefulness of the work if the basis on which you predetermined the contract price was insecure, or if your work specification was not entirely correct. So a decision to choose this form of contract has to be thought about carefully.

Fixed prices are tricky to calculate, as observed in Chapter 3. They work best in situations where 1) the product you require is cut and dried; 2) the work needed to achieve it can be specified accurately and

LETTER OF ENGAGEMENT FOR THE PROVISION OF CONSULTANCY SERVICES

1. This letter sets out the terms and conditions on which ABC Ltd proposes to engage you as an independent contractor to provide consultancy services.

Services
2. The services that you will undertake are the following:
   (a) To read and examine a representative sample of the business tenders produced by ABC Ltd over the past 12 months, together with their accompanying tender documentation, and including both successful and unsuccessful tenders.
   (b) To make an assessment of the quality, impact and business focus of the tenders.
   (c) To produce a report on the findings of the assessment, which shall include recommendations on measures to further develop and strengthen ABC Ltd's tender procedures.

3. You undertake to use all reasonable skill, care and diligence in the provision of these services.

Duration of engagement
4. The period of the engagement is 6 (six) working days. This is to include 0.5 working day for a briefing by a member of ABC Ltd's staff and 5.5 (five and a half) working days for the reading and examination of the tenders and the writing of a report.

5. You will visit the offices of ABC Ltd in Middletown to undertake the reading, examination and assessment of the tenders. It is expected that you will spend 3.5 working days in the offices of ABC Ltd for this purpose.

Timescale
6. The report on the findings of your assessment shall be delivered to the undersigned no later than 25 June 2004.

Payment and allowances
7. In consideration of your services ABC Ltd will provide the following:
   (a) A consultancy fee of £3,000 (three thousand pounds) net of VAT representing a rate of £500 per working day for six working days. The fee covers all preparation, report production and all other work in connection with this engagement. The fee does not include travel time between your office and ABC Ltd's offices in Middletown.
   (b) Reimbursement of the cost of 3 (three) days' accommodation and subsistence in Middletown.

Figure 6.1 *Example of a fixed price contract*

(c) Reimbursement of the cost of return first-class rail travel between your office and Middletown.

8. Once the work is complete to the satisfaction of ABC Ltd, you will submit an invoice for payment of the consultancy fee and reimbursable costs. Original receipts for items claimed as reimbursable costs shall be forwarded together with your invoice. VAT, where applicable, shall be shown separately on the invoice. ABC Ltd will pay all undisputed invoices within 31 days of receipt.

9. You will not receive any compensation or benefits from ABC Ltd other than those expressly provided for in paragraph 7 of this Letter of Agreement.

Indemnification and liability

10. Except to the extent required by law, ABC Ltd shall have no liability for any loss or injury (including death) or damage whatsoever caused or suffered by you that arises out of or in connection with the engagement. In addition you hereby undertake to indemnify ABC Ltd in respect of any claims of whatever kind made against it which arise from any wilful misconduct by you or negligent performance of your duties under this engagement.

Non-disclosure

11. You undertake that, during and after the termination of this Agreement, no disclosure to any third party of any information arising from this Agreement shall be made, except with the prior written permission of ABC Ltd. Any reports or papers prepared by you shall be the property of ABC Ltd, and you hereby assign to ABC Ltd copyright and all associated rights in such reports or papers.

Assignment

12. You shall not, without the prior consent in writing of ABC Ltd, assign, transfer or cause to be transferred or assigned this engagement or any part, share or interest therein to any third party.

Termination of agreement

13. If for any reason ABC Ltd wishes to terminate this Agreement prematurely it may do so by giving you 10 (ten) days' notice in writing.

14. Upon termination payments due to you under this Agreement shall be made for services rendered to the satisfaction of ABC Ltd up to the date of termination. No other payment shall be made.

Figure 6.1 *continued*

Dissatisfaction

15. If for any reason ABC Ltd is dissatisfied with any aspect of the services provided under this Agreement, it may withhold an appropriate sum of money. In this event ABC Ltd will notify you, identifying the particular work with which it is dissatisfied together with the reasons for its dissatisfaction.

Variation

16. This Agreement may be varied by advance agreement in writing between the parties.

Force majeure

17. If the performance of this Contract is delayed, hindered or prevented or is otherwise frustrated by reason of force majeure, which shall mean any event beyond the control of the party affected, then the party so affected shall promptly notify the other in writing.

18. Upon acceptance in writing by the other party of the existence of any such event, or if the other party has failed to respond within 10 (ten) working days, the obligations of both parties shall cease or shall be suspended for an appropriate period of time to be arranged between the parties.

Cessation and suspension of obligations

19. In the event of the cessation of obligations ABC Ltd will pay:
    (a) any sums due or outstanding under the terms of this Contract;
    (b) reimbursement of reasonable expenses directly and necessarily incurred after the relevant date in winding up this Contract.

20. In the event of the suspension of obligations ABC Ltd shall pay any sums due and outstanding under the terms of this Contract at the date of suspension.

Disputes

21. Should you and ABC Ltd be in dispute on the meaning or interpretation of any of the terms of this Agreement, including a failure to agree on an event of force majeure under paragraph 17, the matter shall be referred to an arbitrator to be nominated by the parties or failing such agreement to be agreed by the President of the Law Society of England and Wales on the application of either party, and the decision of the arbitrator shall be final and binding on both parties.

Governing law

22. This contract shall be governed by and construed in accordance with the law of England.

Figure 6.1 _continued_

Signature
23. If the terms and conditions set out in this Letter are acceptable to you please sign and date the attached copy of this Letter where indicated and return that signed copy to me.

For and on behalf of ABC Ltd

Signed ....

Date ....

For and on behalf of *(Consultant)*

Signed ....

Date ....

Yours sincerely

Figure 6.1 *continued*

definitively; 3) the financial risks are small; and 4) the course of the work is relatively proof against changes in priorities and expectations.

In a sense, fixed price contracts use the profit motive to stimulate an efficient performance on the part of the consultants. The more tightly consultants manage resource costs and delivery, the greater the scope for making a profit from the work. There is a downside to this, in that consultants may be encouraged to inflate the price as a hedge against unforeseen changes in the scope of the work, while the need for strict cost control may result in some parts of the work being performed less effectively than they ought to be.

Fixed price contracts have several variants. 'Award fee' contracts and 'incentive' contracts were mentioned in Chapter 3. In both these forms of contract the principal remuneration takes the form of an agreed basic fee to which awards or incentives may be added. Incentive contracts may also provide for consultants to be penalized by having part of the basic fee withheld if they allow time and cost overruns to occur through factors within their control. In another variant, client and consultants agree a target price for the work: if the total fee is less than the target price, the consultants receive an agreed share of the savings; if it is more, the consultants pay an agreed share of the excess.

Uncertainty is the enemy of fixed price contracts. They are rarely suited to research and development work aimed at exploring new possibilities and extending the frontiers of knowledge, where the inputs required and the outputs expected may be hard to define in advance.

For this latter category of work, **time-based contracts** are more appropriate. A target price or ceiling is agreed, based on the consultants' estimate of the total costs likely to be incurred on the work. The consultants are paid for the actual hours worked. In this type of contract it is the client that assumes the inherent risks, paying less if the actual cost is lower than the expected cost but paying more if the work turns out to demand more time and effort. The consultants' fees are related to the amount of their professional input not to their performance, though award fees and incentives may be applied. Clients need to exert firm management if they are to avoid situations in which time-based contracts have continually to be extended before they yield their intended outputs.

Call-off contracts (Figures 6.2, 6.3 and 6.4) are used in situations where a client is likely to require consultancy services on a fairly regular basis. They cover a fixed period – say, two or three years – and enable a client to 'call off' time against the contract as and when work needs to be done. Call-off contracts are sometimes confused with framework agreements but they are not the same. In a framework agreement the client identifies a number of firms that have proved their competence and is able to place orders with them over the period of the agreement without needing to go out to tender each time. Each piece of work up to a prescribed contract value is normally single-sourced, but the framework agreement defines the basic terms and conditions on which contracts are awarded.

Where a project is so complex that its successful delivery depends on the performance of an intricate nexus of consultants and subcontractors, it may be appropriate to use what is termed a **single partnering contract**, which coordinates within an integrated framework the interests of everyone concerned with the work, from the client to individual specialists (Chapter 9). More common in the construction industry, this type of contract involves, among other elements, the development of a project partnering agreement that defines roles, responsibilities, timescales and price formulas as well as procedures for resolving problems. An agreed maximum price is determined before the work starts. Payments can be related to progress measured against key performance indicators, while the contract may offer incentives to promote efficiency savings.

It would be misguided to adopt one or other form of contract simply as a matter of course ('We always use fixed price contracts'). Decide which option will best help you secure the results you want, bearing in mind the degree of risk and the extent to which it is reasonable for risks to be shared between you and the consultants.

AGREEMENT made the (*date*)

PARTIES

(Name of Client) ....

(Name of Consultant) ....

CONTRACT FOR SERVICES

1. The Client appoints the Consultant to provide the following Services for a period of three years beginning on the date of this Agreement.

   a) ....
   b) ....
   c) ....
   d) ....

2. The Client and the Consultant acknowledge that this Agreement is a call-off contract and nothing in this Agreement obliges the Client to place any order with the Consultant for the Services or prevents the Client from placing orders for the Services with persons other than the Consultant.

3. All orders for the Services placed with the Consultant by the Client during the continuance of this Agreement shall be deemed to be placed under the terms and conditions of this Agreement.

4. The rate of payment for the Services ('the Contract Rate') shall be £......... per day exclusive of Value Added Tax, payment to be made subject to the completion of the work to the satisfaction of the Client and subject to the presentation of a VAT invoice.

5. Time spent attending meetings (but not travelling time) and/or discussing the Services by telephone is chargeable to the Client by the Consultant at the Contract Rate.

6. The Contract Rate shall be reviewed by the Client and the Consultant in the month preceding the first and second anniversaries of this Agreement and may be varied as agreed in writing by the Client and the Consultant.

Figure 6.2 *Example of a call-off contract*

7. The Consultant will visit the Client's office as and when the Client shall reasonably require to discuss any work placed or to be placed for the Services.

8. The Client will reimburse the Consultant for the cost of standard-class rail travel to and from any such meetings when invoiced as mentioned in 4.

9. The time required to be spent in travelling between the Consultant's office and the Client's office to attend meetings will not be chargeable to the Client.

10. The Consultant may decline to accept an order for the Services and shall promptly so inform the Client when an order is placed if the Consultant wishes to do so.

PLACING OF ORDERS

11. All orders for the Services shall be given in writing in the first instance or if given verbally initially shall be followed up in writing, which includes fax and e-mail.

12. The written order shall describe fully the work to be done, give the date by which it is to be completed and delivered to the Client, specify any particular requirements the Client may have and contain any other relevant details reasonably necessary to enable the Consultant to provide the Services.

THE CONSULTANT'S UNDERTAKINGS

13. In consideration of this Agreement the Consultant undertakes with the Client as follows:
    a) to provide the Services as an expert consultant and adviser in (name of field);
    b) not to assign this Agreement nor to subcontract the provision of the Services or any part or parts thereof without the written Agreement of the Client;
    c) to indemnify the Client against any claims in respect of employers' liability against the Client or the Consultant by any employees of the Consultant or his or her subcontractor and against any claim for bodily injury or damage to property of third parties.

COPYRIGHT

14. The copyright of all material produced under this Agreement will be and remain the sole and absolute property of the Client and such material will not be used or reproduced elsewhere without the Client's permission.

Figure 6.2 *continued*

15. The Consultant warrants that in delivering the Services he or she will not infringe any copyright intellectual property rights patents or other rights of any other person.

CONFIDENTIALITY

16. All correspondence and other communications between the Client and the Consultant and all material produced under this Agreement by the Consultant are confidential and must not be disclosed to any other person without the Client's permission.

SIGNED on behalf of the Client ....

SIGNED by the Consultant ....

Figure 6.2 *continued*

DRAWING UP A CONTRACT

Though a contract may at first sight seem a bewildering maze of clauses, its terms are normally set out in a logical order:

- what the first party (the client) will do;

- what the second party (the consultants) will do;

- the terms of payment;

- matters relating to the expiry, suspension or termination of the contract;

- warranties (ie assurances) made by the parties;

- indemnities (normally security against or exemption from legal responsibilities);

- general matters related to the performance of the contract or the rights and responsibilities of the parties.

At the bare minimum, the contract should state the following items:

- Who the contract or agreement is between.

■ When the contract comes into effect and when it ends. It is important to make sure the contract is dated as well as signed and witnessed. The date when the contract is entered into normally appears at the start of the document.

■ The work or services to be undertaken and the tasks to be achieved. These points need to be defined as clearly and precisely as possible. Some clients may want to attach the detailed work specification as part of the contract, but this risks introducing elements of inconsistency into the contract, particularly if the client's perception of its requirements has altered since the work specification was developed. If the terms of the successful proposal are identical with the terms of the contract, consider attaching a copy of the proposal.

■ The person in your business or organization who is responsible for giving instructions and receiving reports related to the work.

■ The outcomes or deliverables of the contract – what the consultants will produce for you by way of reports or other results. As emphasized in Chapter 4, it is important to specify the final deliverable that will mark the completion of the work.

■ The timetable for the work, if this has been defined, or the period for which the contract applies.

■ The agreed price, budget or budget ceiling for the work and the basis of its calculation. If the work is to be done on a time charge basis, indicate the number of hours or days you believe it should take. You may wish to add a statement to the effect that no additional fees or sums of money will be payable by you in respect of the agreed terms of the contract or agreement.

■ The categories of expenses that are reimbursable (Chapter 3).

■ Whether or not the agreed price is net of VAT. Normally contracts state the net price.

■ The terms of payment for the work: particularly 1) the timing of payment – ie whether it is on a daily, weekly or monthly basis or related to the achievement of specific tasks and stages; 2) whether an advance payment is to be made (Chapter 3); and 3) whether payment is subject to your valuation of the work (as advised at the end of this chapter).

■ Specific requirements that have to be met if the work is to be accepted as satisfactory. For example, you may require a defined proportion of the consultants' time input or the contract value to be allocated to particular activities, or you may indicate that a particular set of questions is to be answered.

In many contexts the contractual terms for the work will need to be set out in more detail than the basic items listed above. Additional points that may have to be defined in a contract include the following.

Performance of the work

- How many hours there are considered to be in a working day or how many working days in a calendar month.

- The individuals who will do the work and the competencies you require them to possess. You may wish to name individuals in the contract if you consider them key resources for the success of the work.

- A requirement to seek the client's approval of a substitute, if the named individual cannot be made available. Normally a substitute is expected to be at least equal in competence to the named individual.

- Arrangements on your part for monitoring and reviewing the work, assuming its time span allows this.

- A requirement for either side to give the earliest possible notification of any matter that could change the agreed programme of work.

- You may wish to include a 'force majeure' clause to the effect that neither party shall be liable to the other if it is unable to perform any of its obligations in whole or in part owing to causes beyond its reasonable control.

- Stages in the work or events at which progress and performance will be assessed. If time is of the essence, you may want to state this and tie payment to success in meeting agreed targets.

- How progress, performance and the achievement of targets are to be measured – for example, you may wish to define outcomes and verifiable indicators ('By the end of Month 4, not less than 60 per cent of the agreed total of divisional supervisors will be in post').

■ Arrangements to deal with any problems or delays that may occur in the course of the work – for example, the procedures to be followed in notifying and discussing the emergence of problems (Chapter 7).

■ A requirement on the part of the consultants to correct faults or deficiencies in the performance of the work as soon as they are aware of them.

■ The need to maintain the confidentiality of proprietary business information gained about your organization either through the work specification and related documents or in the course of the work. In law, once a contract has terminated, a duty of confidentiality applies only to information that can be categorized as trade secrets or information of a highly confidential nature. Information that may be termed trivia, gained through knowledge acquired in the course of a contract, is not protected. But the borderline between these two categories is often indistinct. If you are concerned about protecting a particular category or item of information, include in the contract a clause that places an obligation on the consultants expressly to maintain the confidentiality of that information. You might also want to require the consultants to keep confidential the fact that you have put work out to tender.

■ Whether a requirement for confidentiality is to remain in effect for a defined period after the termination of the contract.

■ The need for compliance with specific legislation or statutory regulations, for example in the field of health and safety or environmental protection.

■ Arrangements for obtaining necessary approvals, licences and authorizations. Normally this will be identified as part of the consultants' responsibilities.

■ The need for transparency in work records and accounts of expenditure.

■ Requirements for reporting and presentations (Chapter 7).

■ The place where you expect the work or a particular part of it to be performed, if the location is critical to its success. Bear in mind the employment status implications of requiring consultants to work at your premises rather than their offices (Chapter 1).

- The inputs you will provide to facilitate the work (Chapter 4).

- Requirements for the use of specific computer applications and software versions to ensure compatibility with your systems.

- The procedure for dealing with variations from the initial scope of work and the costs of variations (Chapter 7).

- Other specific points related to the particular characteristics of the work.

Management

- The management tasks for which you require the consultants to take responsibility and those for which you will be responsible.

- Arrangements for liaison and communication with the consultants – for example, the frequency of progress meetings.

- The maintenance of assets (eg equipment that you may be providing for the consultants to use), work records and data (eg back-up and storage requirements).

- Incentives for timely delivery or higher-than-standard service levels and penalties for time and cost overruns or deficiencies in service levels.

- A requirement to operate a quality management system for the work or to produce a risk management plan or contingency plan to address possible delays in the delivery of outputs.

- Arrangements for signing-off work and approving expenditure.

- Requirements for the preparation and submission of invoices.

- Whether you propose to retain a defined percentage of the total fee until you have signed the work off as satisfactorily completed.

- Whether subcontractors may be used for parts of the work, and if so any right you may reserve to approve their proposed appointment, the scope of their participation in the work and the terms of their contract with the consultants.

Legalities

- The need to avoid a conflict of interest with business competitors.

- The minimum indemnity to be carried by the consultants' liability insurance.

- The need for the consultants to provide evidence of insurances required by the contract.

- The copyright and ownership of items produced as part of the work. The fact that you are paying the consultants to produce a deliverable does not in itself mean that you own the intellectual property the deliverable represents. Since the law of copyright is complex, copyright issues need to be discussed with the consultants before the work starts and a clear statement of your respective rights needs to be included in the contract.

- The documentation required before bills and invoices can be paid, eg evidence of tax status or a copy of VAT certification.

- An understanding that the consultants will be responsible for meeting any liability for taxes incurred in connection with their work under the contract or agreement.

- A condition that whatever premises and facilities you may provide are not to be used for marketing or business development activities on the part of the consultants.

- What action or actions will constitute a breach of contract.

- Provision to modify or amend the contract if the amendment is made in writing and is signed by both parties.

- Grounds and procedures for early termination of the contract.

- Provisions for the resolution of disputes, mediation and arbitration.

- A statement to the effect that: 1) the contract contains the entire agreement between the parties; 2) there are no other undertakings or conditions in any other agreement whether oral or written; 3) the contract supersedes any prior written or oral agreements between the parties.

Case Study

John R had recently set up in business as a timber importer. To assess the feasibility of a marketing venture, he called in a firm of economics consultants that his lawyer recommended to him.

Following an exchange of e-mails about the proposed work, the firm sent him its standard terms of engagement. These appeared highly biased in favour of the consultants. Among other points, they included clauses that required him to agree that the nature and extent of the feasibility research would be left entirely to their discretion, that he would be liable for all costs and expenses that the consultants deemed it necessary to incur, and that he would engage the consultants for any consequent follow-up work. He wrote to the firm explaining why he was unwilling to accept their terms and asked his lawyer to suggest another firm.

There was a quick response from the consultants. Their managing partner phoned to suggest that John should indicate any changes that he thought would make the agreement fairer. With advice from his lawyer, John shaped the agreement into a more reasonable form, amending in particular the clauses that had looked so troublesome. One or two items had to be negotiated, but the result was a basis that both he and the consultants were able to sign up to.

GUIDELINES TO STEER YOU CLEAR OF PROBLEMS

- If any of the points listed above needs to be spelt out in detail, obtain professional legal advice. In most sectors of consultancy there are specific items and elements, related for example to methods and procedures, that both clients and consultants will need to see defined in unambiguous terms and that may well demand the attention of a lawyer. Try to use a lawyer who has specialist experience of contracts in the relevant field.

- Over the years, your company may have developed a standard form of contract that it uses routinely for consultancy services. It is worth asking a lawyer to review its terms and conditions from time to time, to check first that no significant point has been either omitted or misstated, and second that it is in line with current legislation and practice.

■ If you are drafting a contract, use straightforward language and an uncomplicated form of words. One should not have to read a clause two or three times to work out what it means. Each sentence in a clause should make a single point. The more you clarify and simplify, the more value you add to the contract.

■ Apply terms consistently. This may make for tedious writing, but remember that a contract is meant to be used not read, and it is essential to avoid the ambiguity that will result if you give the same thing different names.

■ If there are terms open to interpretation, make sure they are defined in the contract. Many contracts open with a section listing definitions and interpretations – for example, 'For the purposes of this Agreement, Delivery Plan means the document annexed to this Agreement in which the Consultant has specified in detail the way in which it will deliver the Services, and which may not be altered or amended without the prior written consent of the Company.' Include also a statement to the effect that the headings in the agreement shall not affect its interpretation.

■ Remember that it is pointless to include conditions that are unenforceable. Don't clog up the contract with unnecessary clauses.

■ There are consultants who have a policy of asking their legal advisers and professional liability insurers to review every contract drawn up by a client, so as to ensure that the client is not attempting to transfer to them what they would regard as an unreasonable and inequitable degree of liability.

■ To avoid compromising the independent status of the consultants, as noted in Chapter 1, do not use wording that might imply the existence of an employer/employee relationship between you and the consultants (Figure 1.2). In particular, take care not to write that the consultants will be 'employed', 'controlled' or 'supervised' or that their work will be managed or directed by someone in your organization. The 'status' clause in the US contract reproduced as Figure 6.4 offers a useful form of words.

■ For the same reasons, it is advisable in a contract to refer to the consultants as 'the Company' (as in Figure 6.3) if it is a firm that is providing the services. If the contract is with an individual, it is normal either to use the person's name or to refer to 'the Consultant' or 'the Contractor'. In the latter case, whichever form of words you use, make it clear that the individual works independently of your organization, and that he or she will receive no benefits from your organization other than the fees and expenses provided for in the contract.

Ensuring consultants do not become employees

Care should be taken in the wording of the contract and in the management of the consultant so that an employer/employee relationship is not inadvertently established. Such a relationship may result in your unit becoming liable for various leave and workers' compensation claims.

Some of the characteristics of an employer/employee relationship are:

- the employer has the right to determine, in a detailed way from day to day, how, where and in what manner the employee is to do the assigned work;

- the employer provides all or most of the materials and tools of work;

- fixed specified hours or time of work are prescribed; and

- the employee works for no other person and is required to give the whole of his or her working time to the employer.

(Source: *Guidelines for Achieving the Effective Use of Consultants in the ACT (Australian Capital Territory) Public Service*, Chief Minister's Department and Department of Treasury, January 2001)

- Clauses related to contract variations and change orders (Chapter 7) need to be drafted with particular care. You should define in detail the procedures to be followed on the consultants' part in seeking and obtaining approval for additional work, as well as the means of resolving disagreements about whether the work is within or outside the scope of the services set out in the contract.

- In some jurisdictions, the consultants' proposal becomes part of the contract, once it has been accepted by the client. If significant departures from the terms of the proposal have been agreed during negotiation, identify them in the contract.

■ State that the fee for the work is agreed subject to valuation – in other words, reserve the right not to pay it in full if you are not fully satisfied with the quality of the work. In the same vein, use the phrase 'satisfactory completion' rather than just 'completion', and define what you will require in order to be satisfied.

■ If you are in business you might be tempted to require consultants not to work for any of your competitors, at least for a period after the end of the contract. Resist the temptation: such a requirement might be interpreted as an unlawful restraint of trade.

■ Check the text thoroughly to spot any careless errors or unclear wording. Make sure that the parties to the contract are described accurately and their names spelt correctly.

When you are satisfied with the draft of the contract, send two copies of the finalized document to the consultants for signature and dating, asking for one to be returned to you. Check that the administrative paperwork on your side is ready, and that your accounts unit is aware of the contract. Set up a contract file system, including the work specification, the proposal submitted by the selected consultants and a copy of the contract.

Negotiating with consultants

Negotiation has been described as 'applied common sense'. The objective should be to reach an agreement that is fair both to you and to the consultants and forms a practical and sensible basis for getting the work done:

■ Don't go into a negotiation with the aim of driving a hard bargain and getting the better of the other side. You are more likely to secure the results you want by adopting an approach that is constructive rather than adversarial, aiming to resolve or reconcile differences and searching for solutions that will sustain an effective and amicable working relationship. After all, you would not be negotiating with the consultants if you did not think that they might well be the people best suited to undertake the work.

■ For a negotiation to be successful, each party has to believe it can trust the other's word and that the attitudes presented at the meeting are genuinely intended to achieve a mutually beneficial outcome.

■ Make sure you are well prepared – first, with facts, figures and relevant documentation, and second, with a tactical plan that takes account of the consultants' position and the negotiating options available to the consultants. Weigh up the possible arguments and counter-arguments the consultants may put forward, but look continually for points on which you can agree. You want the consultants to feel you are being firm but reasonable and willing to see matters from their viewpoint too.

■ Identify beforehand any issues that are sufficiently critical to you as to allow no compromise and issues on which you are prepared to make concessions in return for concessions on the part of the consultants. Negotiations rarely result in one side having things all its own way: generally the outcome is a solution developed through discussion, bargaining and give and take.

■ Determine in advance your fall-back position and identify the room for manoeuvre. Make no compromise or concession that has not been planned and thought through before the meeting.

■ In negotiation, as in most other areas of business, listening is more important than talking. Pay careful attention to what the consultants say and listen for signs of room for compromise.

■ Write notes to your colleagues rather than holding whispered conversations, but be careful not to leave your notes lying around on the table during breaks in the meeting.

■ Before you start to discuss issues of price, check back on your budget calculations (Chapter 4) and see if you are still happy with them. You do not want the consultants to be the first to spot errors or underestimates on your part.

■ If there are cost items or resources that you want to challenge ('Why do you need a part-time planner and a project engineer in the team?', 'Why have you estimated £x for other publication expenses?'), ask the consultants to explain what value is added by the item in question and how its cost was calculated.

■ You may have decided that the consultants with whom you are negotiating are the right people for you, but there may be items in their proposal that you do not need or want. Make that point clear and ask them to show how they can reduce their price by pruning their outputs to take account of your priorities.

■ The consultants may assert that the price they have quoted will give them only a marginal return. In that case, ask why they have spent time and effort in pursuing the work to the negotiating table. They may be claiming marginality only to defend themselves from a call to reduce their price.

■ They may try to justify a high price by pointing to elements of the work programme that carry high levels of risk. You should then ask for a commitment from them not to seek to transfer the risk to subcontractors if awarded the contract.

■ Make a realistic assessment of your relative bargaining strengths. Are the skills and services you need in short supply? How hard or easy would it be to find someone equally competent to do the work? How important is your contract likely to be to the consultants?

■ The other side in the negotiation may be a group or consortium of firms. Even though they will usually have nominated one member of the group to be the sole negotiating and contracting party, their views may diverge on matters of detail. If you can detect a lack of unanimity on their side, you may be able to use this to reinforce your own negotiating position.

■ While it is not good practice to reveal one competitor's price to another or to disclose ideas that were part of a competing proposal, there is no reason why you should not try to obtain the maximum advantage from the preferred consultants ('One of the competitors closest to you in price is offering to include the development of control procedures at no extra cost. Can you offer us the same?').

CONTRACT FOR SERVICES

1. This Contract for Services is made on the 2004

between
XYZ Limited
Registered Office: ....

and
John Smith Associates (the Company)
Registered Office: ....

The Company is in business as a provider of consultancy services and has skills and competencies that may be of use to XYZ Limited from time to time.

XYZ Limited and the Company agree that when the Company undertakes services to XYZ Limited it will do so in accordance with the operative provisions of this Contract for Services.

2. OPERATIVE PROVISIONS OF THIS CONTRACT FOR SERVICES

2.1 Services to be undertaken, contract services price, substitution and other matters

2.1.1 This Contract for Services shall commence and thereafter will terminate on the dates stated in Schedule B attached.

2.1.2 Within 30 days of the signing of this Contract for Services, the Company will supply XYZ Limited with a copy of its relevant certificate of incorporation and VAT registration (if applicable) together with relevant bank details.

2.1.3 The Duration of this Contract for Services is as set out in Schedule B, and new Contracts for Services may be negotiated by agreement in writing between the parties.

2.1.4 The Company agrees to provide the services to XYZ Limited set out in Schedule E attached.

2.1.5 The Company agrees to undertake the contract services in a professional manner at all times and to undertake the services in the capacity of a specialist.

2.1.6 XYZ Limited shall not control, nor have any right of control as to how the Company is to perform the contract services. XYZ Limited recognizes that the Company offers specialist services at a high level of expertise and that as such the Company cannot be instructed as to the manner in which the contract services are to be performed.

Figure 6.3 *Example of a call-off contract*

2.1.7 The Company undertakes that it will devote such time, attention, skill and ability as the contract services require.

2.1.8 The Company will use its own experience and initiative in judging how the contract services are to be completed and will have flexibility as to the hours worked on location, but will nonetheless assist XYZ Limited by making all reasonable attempts to work with an overall agreed deadline, will observe Health and Safety regulations and will comply with all reasonable operational requirements relating to working hours and security.

2.1.9 The Company, its directors, employees or consultants are not obliged to seek permission from XYZ Limited to leave a location at any time.

2.1.10 The Contract Price for the contract services will be negotiated and agreed as between XYZ Limited and the Company and this will be detailed in Schedule C attached.

2.1.11 XYZ Limited will pay the Company's contract services price (plus VAT if appropriate) in accordance with the rates set out in Schedule C solely against the presentation of an invoice and a signed timesheet.

2.1.12 Payment will be made into a bank account nominated by the Company within 30 working days of receiving an invoice from the Company.

2.1.13 Both XYZ Limited and the Company agree that this is a Contract for Services essentially in respect of specialist services only.

2.1.14 The Company will prepare invoices for all contract services undertaken on a frequency confirmed in Schedule D.

2.2 Financial risk

2.2.1 Both the Company and XYZ Limited are obliged to honour any agreed contract services price, unless both parties renegotiate the contract services price.

2.2.2 In the event that the contract services are carried out by the Company, its servants or agents, consultants, substitutes or hired assistants in a defective manner and/or otherwise than in accordance with the skills and abilities of a specialist the Company will take all reasonable steps as soon as practicable to remedy and/or correct the contract services at its own expense and in its own time. In the event that the Company fails to remedy and/or correct the contract works within a reasonable time XYZ Limited will be entitled to remedy and/or correct the contract services at the Company's expense. All such expense incurred by XYZ Limited will be reimbursed and/or paid by the Company to XYZ Limited on demand.

Figure 6.3 *continued*

2.2.3 The Company confirms that it is qualified to perform the contract of works.

2.2.4 The Company, its directors, employees or consultants will not be entitled to receive sick pay in any circumstances from XYZ Limited.

2.2.5 Either party can terminate this Contract for Services by giving the other four weeks' written notice.

2.2.6 The Company is not entitled to partake in any grievance procedure with XYZ Limited and as an independent company is not entitled to any employment law rights.

2.2.7 XYZ Limited is not obliged to offer ongoing contracts or contract services to the Company nor is the Company obliged to accept such contracts or contract services if offered. The Company is not obliged to make its services available. Specifically both parties declare that they do not wish to create or imply any mutuality of obligations whatsoever during the course of this Contract for Services or during any period when contract services are not available.

2.2.8 The Company accepts it has legal risk in respect of professional indemnity, public liability and employers' liability and will therefore pay the costs of such insurance premiums and maintain adequate cover at all times.

2.2.9 XYZ Limited reserves the right to offset any losses sustained as a result of the Company's actions, breach or negligence, from the Company's fees.

2.2.10 The Company is not entitled to receive any company benefits from XYZ Limited or partake in any pension scheme run by XYZ Limited.

2.3 Freedom of the company to undertake other works

2.3.1 The Company is free to undertake other Contracts for Services for other parties at any time, either before, after or concurrently with this Contract for Services, provided they are not in conflict with the services being provided under this Contract.

2.3.2 XYZ Limited acknowledges and agrees that it does not have first call on the services of the Company and cannot require the Company to give XYZ Limited any priority over another client.

2.3.3 The Company may advertise its services in any way it sees fit and XYZ Limited shall not raise any objection.

2.3.4 The Company may use a business trading name.

Figure 6.3 *continued*

2.4 Confidentiality

2.4.1 The Company undertakes that it and its directors, employees, consultants and substitutes shall keep in the strictest confidence all details of trade secrets and confidential information that may come into its possession during the completion of the Contract's services.

2.4.2 At the end of the term of this Contract for Services the Company undertakes to deliver to XYZ Limited all documents relating to the contract services that contain trade secrets or confidential information relating to XYZ Limited business.

2.4.3 All copyright and other intellectual property right in all work, including all work of a preparatory or design nature, or developed or created from such work in performing the contract services, shall be deemed to be the undisputed property of XYZ Limited.

2.4.4 In the event of XYZ Limited supplying to the Company any material in which XYZ Limited owns the copyright or any other intellectual property rights the material will be supplied by the Client under a licence, which may be terminated by the Client on immediate notice, to use the same or any part thereof as the Client shall in its absolute discretion deem fit.

2.5 Taxation and national insurance

The Company as an independent business is responsible for its own (corporation) tax.

2.6 Business organization

2.6.1 The Company will at all times represent itself as an independent business and will in no circumstances represent itself or hold itself out as a representative, servant or employee of XYZ Limited. The Company hereby acknowledges it is in business on its own account and is not part and parcel of XYZ Limited's business, or any other business.

2.6.2 The Company will maintain at its own cost appropriate independent office accommodation, telephone system, mobile telephone, fax facility and e-mail facility.

2.7 Intention of the parties

2.7.1 Both parties agree and intend that this legal relationship is one of contracting for independent specialist services and specifically is not a relationship of master and servant or employer and employee.

Figure 6.3 *continued*

2.7.2 The parties to this Contract for Services specifically confirm that it is their understanding and intention that this Contract and this Contract alone is the 'contractual arrangements' and 'circumstances'.

2.8 Legal advice and other matters

2.8.1 Both parties hereby acknowledge that they have had an opportunity to take independent legal advice before signing this Contract for Services.

2.8.2 Both parties acknowledge that their contractual relationship is governed by this Contract for Services as a legally binding agreement.

2.8.3 Both parties acknowledge that this Contract for Services is the whole agreement governing the contractual relationship between them, except where this Contract for Services allows for specific negotiations under Clause 2.2.1.

2.8.4 Words referring to the masculine are to include the feminine.

2.8.5 This Contract is governed by the laws of England, and subject to the jurisdiction of the English Courts.

2.8.6 In the event of any dispute or difference arising between the parties to this Contract from or in connection with this Contract or its performance, construction or interpretation, such dispute shall be referred to arbitration by a single arbitrator in accordance with the provisions of the Arbitration Act 1996, or any amendments thereto, such arbitrator being either an independent solicitor or accountant appointed by agreement between the parties or, in default of agreement, by the President for the time being of the Law Society or the President for the time being of the Royal Institute of Chartered Accountants upon the application of either party. The decision of any such arbitrator shall be final and binding on the parties.

The Parties agree and intend to be bound by this Contract for Services.

For XYZ Limited:　　　　　For the Company:

Signed: _____　　Signed: _____

Date: _____　　　Date: _____

CONTRACT FOR SERVICES

SCHEDULE A THE COMPANY

Name

Figure 6.3 *continued*

Address

Phone Number

Company Registration Number

VAT Registration Number

Contact Name

SCHEDULE B DURATION OF CONTRACT WORKS

Commencement Date

End Date

SCHEDULE C CONTRACT SERVICES PRICE

XYZ Limited will pay the Company in line with the schedule below for the services of .... This contract services price is based on working the number of days identified in each of the nominated periods.

Period	Dates	Days Worked	Percentage Call-Off	Value
Total				

SCHEDULE D INVOICING FREQUENCY

Invoices are to be submitted in line with Schedule C.

SCHEDULE E THE CONTRACT SERVICES

The Scope of Works is detailed below:
....
....

Figure 6.3 *continued*

Chapter 1 referred to the possibility that a contract for an individual's professional services may, in certain circumstances, be interpreted by the tax authorities as disguised employment. The call-off contract in this example has been designed on the basis of advice from a solicitor and an accountant specifically to avoid such an interpretation. For example, the individual consultant is referred to as 'the Company'; it is made clear that the client is not in a position to exercise control or supervision over the consultant, or to instruct the consultant how to go about the work (clauses 2.1.6 and 2.1.8); the status of the consultant as an independent business that handles its own tax affairs is emphasized (2.5); and the freedom of the consultant to work when and where he or she chooses is implicit.

Figure 6.3 *continued*

CONSULTANT'S AGREEMENT

This Agreement effective (date) is made between.................. (referred to as 'the Company') and.................. ('the Consultant').

WHEREAS, the Consultant has acquired extensive knowledge of and experience in the business as conducted by the Company;

WHEREAS, the Company desires to obtain the benefit of the Consultant's knowledge and experience by retaining the Consultant, and the Consultant desires to accept such position, for the term and upon the other conditions hereinafter set forth;

NOW, THEREFORE, in consideration of the premises and of the mutual agreements contained herein, the parties agree as follows:

Term:
This Agreement shall commence on (date) and shall terminate on (date) (the 'Consulting Term') unless earlier terminated for any reason by either party hereto upon thirty (30) days' prior written notice.

Consultations:
During the Consulting Term the Consultant shall make himself available at reasonable times to provide business consulting services to the officers, directors and other representatives of the Company as reasonably requested by the Chief Executive Officer of the Company (hereafter, the 'Executive') or his designees and the Company will provide the Consultant with reasonable access to the facilities and senior management.

Figure 6.4 *Example of a call-off contract (US)*

156

The Consultant shall not represent the Company, its Board of Directors, its officers or any other members of the Company in any transactions or communications, nor shall the Consultant make claim to do so unless authorized by the Executive or his designees.

The Consultant agrees to consult with the Executive or his designees in the event a situation arises in which his opinion, if expressed, or his actions, if taken, could possibly affect the interests or reputation of the Company. While the Consultant is free at all times to express his opinions he agrees that any such opinion(s) expressed or actions taken are his and not those of the Company and, if not specifically authorized by the Company in writing, may, at the option of the Company, result in termination of this Agreement.

It is understood that this Agreement will require the Consultant to provide consultation regarding strategic planning initiatives and other aspects of the Company's business which may require the Company to disclose to the Consultant secret, proprietary and confidential information concerning the Company and its business affairs. The Consultant also acknowledges that, during the course of his employment with the Company prior to the date hereof, he has been entrusted with certain personnel, business, financial, technical and other information and material which are the property of the Company and which involve confidential information of the Company and the Company's employees. The Consultant agrees to maintain the confidentiality of all Company trade secrets, proprietary and confidential information.

The Consultant agrees that all inventions, developments or improvements made by the Consultant, either alone or in conjunction with others, at any time or any place during the term of the Consultant's assignment with the Company, whether or not reduced to writing or practice during the term, which relate to the business in which the Company or any subsidiary or affiliate is engaged or in which the Company or any subsidiary or affiliate intends to engage, shall be the exclusive property of the Company. The Consultant shall promptly disclose any such invention, development or improvement to the Company, and, at the request and expense of the Company, shall assign all of the Consultant's rights to the same to the Company.

Upon termination of the assignment, the Consultant shall deliver to the Company all drawings, manuals, letters, notes, notebooks, reports, computer files and all other materials (including all copies of such materials), relating to such confidential information or the business of the Company which are in the possession or under the control of the Consultant.

Compensation:
For the performance of the services to be rendered to the Company pursuant to the terms of this Agreement, the Company shall pay the Consultant Seven Thousand Dollars ($7,000) per month on a monthly basis. The Consultant shall

Figure 6.4 *continued*

submit an itemized statement of services performed during any particular month by the sixth (6th) day of the next succeeding month. The amount shall be paid to the Consultant within fifteen (15) business days of the Company's receipt of such statement.

Expenses:
In the event that the Consultant is required, in connection with the performance of services hereunder, to incur business expenses, eg travel and lodging, the Company shall reimburse the Consultant for all reasonable and necessary expenses that have been approved in advance by the Executive or his designees. In connection with such expenses, the Consultant shall submit to the Company documentation substantiating same, eg receipts, and shall be reimbursed within fifteen (15) business days of the Company's receipt of an invoice together with such substantiating documentation.

Time Devoted To Work:
In the performance of the services, the time the Consultant is to work on any given day will be entirely within the Consultant's control and the Company will rely upon the Consultant to put in such amount of time as is reasonably necessary to fulfil the spirit and purpose of this agreement.

Status:
The Consultant is engaged as an independent contractor and shall be treated as such for all purposes, including but not limited to Federal and State taxation, withholding, unemployment insurance, and workers' compensation. It is understood that the Company will not withhold any amounts for payment of taxes from the compensation of the Consultant and that the Consultant will be solely responsible to pay all applicable taxes from said payments, including payments owed to any employees and subagents of the Consultant. The Consultant will not be considered an employee of the Company for any purpose.

Representations and Warranties:
The Consultant will make no representations, warranties, or commitments binding the Company without the Executive's prior written consent.

Employment of Others:
The Company may from time to time request that the Consultant arrange for the services of others. All costs to the Consultant for those services will be paid by the Company but in no event shall the Consultant employ others without the prior authorization of the Company.

No Adequate Remedy:
The Consultant understands that if the Consultant fails to fulfil the Consultant's obligations under this Agreement, the damages to the Company would be very difficult to determine. Therefore, in addition to any other rights or

Figure 6.4 *continued*

remedies available to the Company at law, in equity, or by statute, the Consultant hereby consents to the specific enforcement of this Agreement by the Company through an injunction or restraining order issued by an appropriate court.

Modification:
This Agreement may be modified or amended only in writing and signed by both the Executive and the Consultant.

Governing Laws:
The laws of (state) will govern the validity, construction and performance of this Agreement. Any legal proceeding related to this Agreement must be litigated in an appropriate state or federal court, and both the Company and the Consultant hereby consent to the exclusive jurisdiction of such court for this purpose.

Construction:
Wherever possible, each provision of this Agreement will be interpreted so that it is valid under the applicable law. In the event any portion of this Agreement is declared invalid, the remainder of this Agreement also will continue to be valid.

Waivers:
No failure or delay by either the Company or the Consultant in exercising any right or remedy under this Agreement will waive any provision of the Agreement. Nor will any single or partial exercise by either the Company or the Consultant of any right or remedy under this Agreement preclude either of them from otherwise or further exercising these rights or remedies, or any other rights or remedies granted by any law or any related document.

Notices:
All notices and other communications required or permitted under this Agreement shall be in writing and sent by registered first-class mail, postage prepaid, addressed to the party's last known business address and shall be effective five days after mailing to the address stated at the beginning of this Agreement. These addresses may be changed at any time by like notice.

The parties to this Agreement have read this Agreement and understand it.

(Signatures and dates)

Figure 6.4 *continued*

7

How do I keep track of the work?

BEFORE THE WORK STARTS

Between the signing of the contract and the start of work, you will find it useful to have a further meeting or at least a phone conversation with your consultants to confirm that the necessary arrangements are in place both on their side and on yours. A key point to make clear to them is exactly who will be responsible for giving them instructions and whom they are to contact on day-to-day matters. This will normally be one and the same person, but it may well be someone other than the signatory of the contract – and it is important not to have more than one person telling the consultants what to do!

At the same time, confirm who on their side will deal with any questions you may have. Is it the individual doing the work or a team leader or a manager in the consultancy firm? The meeting also provides an opportunity to remind the consultants of the importance of keeping to schedule and delivering results on time, particularly if there are deadlines that you as a client have to meet.

If the consultants will be working on your business premises or with the staff of your organization, there are a number of preparatory steps that can help get the contract off to a good start:

- Follow the advice in Chapter 1 about bringing your staff onside and engaging their cooperation.

- Make sure that whatever data, documents, contacts or other initial inputs you have agreed to provide are ready.

- See that any necessary arrangements are in place for the consultants to gain access to your premises. If identification and security tags are needed, they should be available on the day work is due to start.

- Inform the consultants about the work locations of people they will need to talk to and the whereabouts of office facilities and services, and provide them with either dedicated working space or a sufficient number of 'hot desks'.

- If your office has a reception desk, let the people who staff it know that consultants are working with you and may need to receive phone calls or faxes. It may also be useful to give the consultants e-mail access via an office intranet.

- Consultants may sometimes submit invoices under a company name that differs from the one you are used to. Check how they propose to bill you and make sure your accounts staff recognize the name and the work it relates to.

It can be helpful to launch the contract with an induction meeting at which the consultants are introduced to your key staff and receive a briefing on the objectives of the work and your organization's business environment, as well as practical guidance about contacts and access to services and data. The handouts at the meeting might include a 'briefing pack' containing a copy of the work specification and material such as background papers, guidelines on the use of office systems, notes on 'where to find what' and a staff list.

ONCE THE WORK IS UNDER WAY

Keep a record of whatever discussions you have with the consultants, in particular any further instructions you may give them and any requests they may make for you to approve changes from the way things were defined in the work specification. If points are raised over the phone, make an immediate note of the conversation, recording the date and time and quoting so far as possible the exact words used by the consultants. This requires a methodical approach on your part and may seem an unnecessary chore, but it will prove its value if there is ever any argument about what was said by whom and when.

The key point to keep in mind in tracking the work is that _you_ are in charge, not the consultants. It is your objectives that must set the pace. If the consultants work slowly or casually, they are likely to be wasting the money you are paying them. Like the rest of us, consultants can catch colds and face problems in their personal lives, but as professionals they ought to be able to find a way round these difficulties and not make them their clients' problems.

Few consultancy assignments go exactly to plan. Unless the job is small, short and straightforward, there will always be things that do not work out as we had expected and could have been done sooner or better. It's one of the penalties of having work done by human beings. We were promised delivery on Friday but it comes in on Monday; we thought we would be charged x but a bill comes in for x plus a few per cent. In most cases we live with it. If we are sensible, we look at the results to judge whether we have still received value for money. If we need to phone the consultants, it will probably be to inquire about the reasons for the delay or the difference in cost, not to berate them for incompetence.

Contracts begin to turn sour when a day's delay extends to a week, when the budget starts to wear thin with little to show for the expenditure, and when we are not told what is causing the problem. The later we learn about difficulties, the less chance there will be to resolve them, get the work back on course and achieve the results we want. This is why it is so important to keep track of the work as it is taking shape, particularly when it has to be done to a tight deadline and a limited budget.

This principle applies to both fixed price contracts and time-based contracts (Chapter 6). Even though the consultants have assumed the financial risk in a fixed price contract, you will want to know that the money you are paying is being applied efficiently to achieve your business objectives. It will be unhelpful to you if work is not delivered on time because the consultants are mismanaging resources.

VIEWPOINT

'How the consultants are briefed in the first place is critical. The best results are always achieved when consultants are working to a clear and precise brief. It also means we are less likely to have our money wasted through consultants going off on the wrong tack.

'The way consultants are selected is very important. I think it is generally best done by competitive tender. When reading proposals, we often find that the quantity of paper is inversely proportional to the quality of the document. We ignore descriptions of the firm and lengthy CVs, which, together with devices such as double spacing and single-sided printing, can make the proposal look much more impressive – until the front cover is opened and the text read!

'Before appointing management consultants, be clear about who exactly is going to do the work, as against those who may be fielded at interviews and meetings to win the contract. We find that the lead consultants are generally good, but the staff who support them can be variable and they rarely have experience in our sector of business. Establish how much input from a director or partner you will be paying for, and make sure you obtain value for this.

'We are always suspicious of consultants who seek vast amounts of information and data from us. That usually seems to mean that the consultants simply intend to perform some relatively basic analysis. We are quite capable of doing that ourselves. What we are really paying for is original thinking and a different perspective. This doesn't mean to say, of course, that there isn't a certain amount of basic information and context that consultants will need if they are to do their job. But we are engaging them for something more.

'Think about the impact of consultants on the work of your own staff. Consultants can end up generating as much work as if the job were being done in-house!

'Establish clear arrangements for guiding and steering the work. If the job is not too short, a quick interim report is often useful in giving us a view about whether the work is going in the right direction and is aimed at the questions it is meant to answer.

'We won't sign off a contract if we think consultants need to do more work to follow up points that are not absolutely clear in the advice they are giving us. Sometimes we hold back money from the budget against this possibility.

'Management consultants can often find themselves working on jobs that might raise conflicts of interest – for example, work for companies that are part of a competitor group. We have to take it on trust that "Chinese walls" work effectively in these organizations, but that is often difficult to establish.

'One further point: be on the lookout for consultants producing conclusions and recommendations that suggest, ever so subtly, that we need to commission more work from them!'

(Consultancy manager, retail stores group)

MONITORING PERFORMANCE AND PROGRESS

Checking performance is critically important if the work involves a challenging delivery schedule and if it is the first time you have used those particular consultants. You do not want to find, for example, at the end of Month 4 that the consultants have done only as much as they planned to achieve by the end of Month 2. On a positive note, monitoring the work can yield benefits for the consultants by providing early signals of emerging problems, in time for them to address the situation. The case for tracking progress and performance on time-based contracts is self-evident, since you will want to make sure consultants are not dragging their heels, particularly if you have yet to discover their quality and reliability.

Some types of work are performed against a timetable of outputs or schedule of deliverables that offer a yardstick for progress and achievement. Other types of work may have few if any interim products – perhaps only a final outcome after weeks of effort. If the job you are having done falls into the latter category, don't be content simply to let the consultants get on with things. Make sure they know you expect to be kept in the picture about how the work is going, how much has been accomplished in relation to the budget spent, what conclusions they are reaching, how far they have got in analysing a problem, and so forth.

It is not so much the process of keeping you informed that is important as ensuring you have adequate information on which to base your management decisions in the course of the contract. This requirement is a point that should have been written into the contract, and it needs to be confirmed at the start of work. Good consultants know that clients like to see what they are getting for their money, so staying in close touch is in their interests too.

Keeping track of the work is largely a matter of maintaining an effective dialogue with your consultants – not just communicating (which can be a one-directional flow) but sharing and exchanging information, ensuring that the people working on the contract understand your objectives and requirements and that you understand what they are doing and why. The measures you need to take will depend on your knowledge of the consultants and the way they work, on the technical demands of the contract and its timescale, and on the levels of risk attached to the contract.

In many situations a light touch is all that is needed so far as monitoring is concerned. Jobs that are straightforward and short may call only for a meeting or two or an exchange of e-mails to check how the work is going and how the budget is being spent. Complex and long-term assignments warrant a systematic process of quality management that will allow you to review the course of the work and measure progress in achieving targets. Make sure, though, that the scale and timing of your contract monitoring activity do not put unreasonable pressures on the consultants' workload, particularly at critical stages in an assignment.

Large corporate organizations normally have standard procedures for gauging the performance of consultancy assignments and matching outputs to budget expenditure. The future of the managers who are accountable for engaging consultants may depend on how well or badly a contract turns out. What they need to gain is a reputation for delivering contracts successfully, not for letting them run into problems or spin out of control. But even where you are not obliged to apply management controls, it is in your interests to stay informed about the progress of the work and leave consultants in no doubt about the professional standards expected from them. You will not make the best of a consultancy relationship if you are resentful about the size of the bills you receive and unaware of the work done to justify them.

Whatever the scope and scale of the work, there are basic questions that you need to be able to answer:

■ Are the consultants doing what you asked them to do?

■ Are they delivering on time and keeping to the budget?

■ How good are the results they are achieving?

- Do you have a satisfactory working relationship with them? Do they show commitment and an honest concern for your interests?

- Do their bills look reasonable for the work they have completed? Are they giving value for money?

Some of the answers to these questions may come from day-to-day contact with the consultants, especially if they are working in your offices or calling in regularly. Body language, reactions and chance remarks in the course of a conversation can tell you a lot. Most people can instantly sense even a slight reserve or lack of confidence, the feeling that something is not quite right. But informal contacts on their own are not enough. The contractual relationship between you and the consultants is a formal matter and its performance needs to be recorded through progress meetings as outlined here. Where the consultants are working at a distance, regular progress meetings are an essential means of monitoring both the broad direction the work is taking and the practical details of its delivery.

Progress meetings

These meetings may be scheduled at regular intervals throughout a contract or timed to coincide with the completion of stages in the work programme or the production of specific deliverables. They serve several purposes:

- recording the status of the work to date and progress toward achieving targets;

- reviewing the performance of specific tasks and activities;

- identifying points on which the consultants may not be complying with the terms of the contract;

- checking how the work completed matches the budget spent;

- obtaining early warning of problems that either side may be encountering – in particular, logistical factors that might cause an overrun of time and cost – and agreeing ways to resolve these issues;

- defining adjustments to the work programme in response to changes in your requirements or in the context of the work;

- identifying any technical points that may need further exploration and discussion;

- confirming working arrangements and forms of communication – for example, the use of e-mails or the Internet, the formatting of data and reports, and compatibility in hardware, operating systems and software;

- identifying matters that may require urgent decisions on your part.

Consultants may be asked to provide written reports for discussion at these meetings. One item of information you are likely to find useful is an itemized breakdown of costs showing just how much has been spent on what. But take care not to focus on the minutiae of project management.

The word 'meeting' may conjure up an image of 10 people sitting round a table all morning. But meetings need not be like that. You will get a better result if you keep them short and to the point, and limit the numbers on your side to one or two people who have a key role to play in the discussion and who are in contact with the day-to-day conduct of the work. Prepare a clear agenda and chair the meeting, so that the consultants are responding to matters raised by you. Make sure you are well prepared with all the relevant documents and data. If you have to negotiate a point, you will need to have your arguments, fallback positions and compromise possibilities worked out in advance. Produce a note of the meeting, indicating actions to be taken and the persons responsible for them, and send a copy to the consultants.

Outside this schedule it is better not to call formal meetings unless they are really necessary: having to attend meetings is likely to be expensive both for you and for the consultants.

Management reports

Consultants engaged on long-term or large-scale assignments are normally required to document their work through a series of management reports to the client. In deciding what reports you will need and when, the factors to consider include:

- the nature and complexity of the assignment: intricate or innovative processes may have to be explained in detail;

- your need for information and your capacity to act on it;

- any requirement for the consultants to maintain an audit trail;

- the pressures of the work timetable and related decision points – for example, the need to fulfil statutory requirements, to meet deadlines set externally, to match the end of financial periods or the frequency of board or committee meetings.

For each report there are several points to be specified, either in the contract or in related instructions:

- the number of copies to be produced;

- the required content;

- whether the document is to be submitted in hard copy, electronic format or both;

- the date when the document is to be submitted;

- whether you want draft copies to be sent to managers within your organization.

One type of management report you will find particularly useful is an inception report, as noted in Chapter 4. Though consultants may have included in their proposal a programme of work to indicate how they would go about the contract, this will in most instances be based on their interpretation of your work specification and from such insights as they may gain in the course of preparing their approach. Only when they have actually got down to work will they be in a position to check out their assumptions and to see your requirements in a fully informed perspective. An inception report is the means of presenting this material. It typically includes:

- a detailed work programme, perhaps with method statements and a critical path network;

- an indication of the scope and timing of any additional technical input or other items that may be needed, eg surveys or tests;

- a statement of any technical or management points still to be decided.

As the term implies, the inception report is produced at or near the start of the work. On long-term assignments, it is customary for clients to require an inception report to be submitted within one to three months of the start date or the date of contract signature. Even on a shorter time span, there are clear benefits to be obtained from having the consultants produce a report of this nature, if it is at all feasible.

When invoices come in

- Does the invoice identify clearly the work to which it relates?
- Is the submission of the invoice in line with the payment terms defined in the contract or letter of engagement?

- Is the amount that is claimed explained? If the contract is based on time charges, does the invoice include the amount of time worked and the applicable charge rate?

- Is the invoice accurate and arithmetically correct?

- If VAT has been charged, is it indicated correctly on the invoice? Does the invoice show the consultant's VAT registration number, the VAT amount and the percentage? These details are important if you are a business registered for VAT and so in a position to reclaim the tax.

- Is the invoice accompanied by receipts or other documentation that may have been specified in the contract?

The client was a small business. Its accounts staff were efficient and made a point of paying invoices within 15 days of receiving them. But this was not fast enough for some of its freelance consultants. One particular consultant whose cash flow was chronically intermittent and who survived on a perilously narrow margin had cultivated the habit of calling in at the accounts office about a week after submitting his invoice to try to persuade them to get his cheque signed just that bit sooner – 'I just happened to be passing and thought I'd look in.' Ideally he would have liked to walk out of the office with a cheque in his hand.

As a device to excuse his persistence and win sympathy he used to conjure up on these occasions the picture of a hungry and desperate family. 'I see those eight little faces looking up at me and asking "Daddy, are we going to eat today?" "You will", I say, "if the nice lady in accounts gives me a cheque."' There came a day when he made a subtle change in the story and talked about nine children, hoping to underline the pathos of his situation. 'We'll post the cheque to you,' said the accounts lady. The cheque arrived the next day, together with a leaflet about birth control.

WHY DO THINGS GO WRONG?

First of all, you need to be sure that things really are going wrong, and that the problem is not caused by the way you have chosen to work with the consultants. As observed in Chapter 4, they may make less progress than you had expected not through a lack of competence or application, but simply because of difficulties inherent in the technical content of the work or in its environment.

Don't necessarily regard this as failure on the part of the consultants. It is in your interests for them to overcome problems quickly, so you stand to gain by seeing whether you can help them in this, perhaps by providing additional information or other inputs to the work. Then again, you may have altered the scope or content of the work without recognizing the implications for the consultants' workload. It is possible also that your attention has become so focused on one part of the work where there are delays that you are failing to notice other parts that are ahead of schedule. So check that you are not the main part of the problem!

The measures outlined in Chapter 4 as ways of reducing the risk of running into problems may seem largely common sense, but often they are ignored and consultancy work fails to deliver its intended benefits for reasons that more forethought and better planning might have prevented. You are left with the consequences – an overspent budget, overdue deliverables, underperformance, poor quality, impractical or irrelevant results, a relationship that starts in cooperation and ends in conflict.

When things go wrong, there is rarely a single cause. This is one reason why you may receive different answers from different people when you try to get to the root of the problem. Looking at the history of an assignment, one can often trace a sequence of errors and mishaps, each of which could have been sorted out at the time, that were allowed to build up into the equivalent of a motorway collision in the fog. And the fault rarely if ever lies with just one side. Clients are often just as much to blame as consultants. If they take on consultants without knowing what they want from them, without having an adequate work specification, a well-drafted contract or a clear definition of responsibilities, they are simply asking for headaches.

But precautions at the contract stage can take you only so far. Difficulties may emerge only after the consultants have started work, and they often come as a total surprise:

- Though you are convinced that the work specification made your requirements crystal clear, the consultants may seem to have a different understanding of what you want. When you look back through the specification and the contract, you may find that they do not in fact contain the points you imagined were there, and that the requirement in question was something you thought of after the contract was signed but never got round to communicating to the consultants.

- Your ideas about what can be achieved within the agreed time span and budget may turn out to be quite unrealistic, but you may be slow to acknowledge misplaced expectations.

- You may, for one reason or another, not be giving the consultants all the information they need to satisfy your requirements. Remember that their work may depend to a large extent on the data you make available to them: normally they will not be able to search through your files to get the full picture. With limited data they can deliver only limited results.

- Your staff and the consultants' personnel may be ill matched in terms of perceptions of competence. If your staff feel they know much less than the consultants, they may defer to them on issues that ought to be questioned. If they feel they know more than the consultants, they may resent their presence and treat them with scepticism. Either way, the outcome will be a damaged working relationship.

- Flexibility may be lacking on either side. Consultants may try to import a standard solution that is part of their methodological toolkit but does not fulfil your needs. You may be unprepared to adapt your expectations to new ideas or changes in the context of the work.

■ If the consultants' work involves change or restructuring within your organization, staff may view the process as something that is being done to them from outside and may react badly to it, rather than seeing it as an initiative in which they have a personal stake.

■ Temperaments and schools of thought may clash. You or the consultants may not possess the interpersonal skills to resolve disputes or prevent them hampering the work.

■ The senior staff on your or the consultants' side who discuss the assignment at management meetings may be entirely unaware of problems that are blatantly obvious to the people doing the work. For various reasons, problems can go unreported until the situation becomes so critical that emergency action is the only recourse.

■ In some cases there is a correlation between the pace at which consultants work and the speed with which their invoices are paid. Of course, it helps if consultants submit their invoices promptly and correctly. Accounts departments and their administrative processes can have an unrecognized but significant impact on the dynamics of an assignment!

■ In a business environment, consultants may be required not only to work together with client staff in a joint team but to manage them throughout the course of a project. This form of working relationship is vulnerable to strains and tensions that can easily distract people from its essential purpose, particularly if the consultants lack an in-depth knowledge of the business. Claims about 'integrated teams' or 'partnership working' are one thing; putting these concepts into practice is quite another. Good working relationships cannot be mandated in a contract. They can only evolve through the application of professional respect, trust and sensitivity – and nurturing them may take almost as much effort as the technical side of a project.

The symptoms of a problem may be clear, but you need to identify accurately the factors that are contributing to it.

Feedback from a wide range of colleagues who have used consultancy support, particularly in systems implementation projects, reveals consistent themes of superficiality, inappropriate models and failure to understand the nature of our business. This is an issue in finding external support not only for student system projects but also for related projects such as financials where an understanding of student finance is essential to adequately meet user requirements. A common feature of 'consultancy-led' projects is that they attempt to shoehorn clients into their own standard template and they can often go a long way off track before the approach is challenged. Realistically you can't always blame them for this. It is inevitable they will have standardized approaches and it is up to us to ensure we understand the models they are using and challenge them where we know that higher education is different.

You do have to remember that this is a commercial relationship. In a good project it won't feel that way; the consultants will be part of your team and helping you achieve your goals. However, if things aren't going so well, don't be afraid to question the approach. The consultancy may have a vested interest in prolonging projects either by belated changes of approach or, in the worst cases, ongoing consultancy support for a live system which is effectively a square peg in a round hole. Most consulting firms will argue they would not risk their reputation by involvement in such projects. Experience, however, shows otherwise. It is, after all, very easy to blame the sector for its naivety or un-businesslike approach whilst continuing to dispatch the invoices.

(Source: Dr Gill Ferrell, *Old Wine, New Labels? Managing Consultancy Input to Projects in the Education Sector*, JISC Centre of Expertise in the Planning and Implementation of Information Systems, Northumbria University, February 2003)

WHAT CAN YOU DO TO PUT MATTERS RIGHT?

There are several measures that can work together to help you succeed in this area of contract management:

- Look for opportunities to enlist the involvement and cooperation of the staff of your organization, perhaps as part of joint teams that can help to test approaches, match them to your needs and start to implement solutions. Don't keep staff at a distance from the work: get them on board.

- Promote a working environment in which there is a climate of frank and open dialogue between you and the consultants, so that problems can be flagged up early and solutions arrived at jointly.

- Use regular progress meetings as an opportunity to recognize problems and difficulties.

- Establish an agreed procedure for resolving concerns and differences of view. This procedure may be specified in the contract or defined in related documents.

- Develop a contingency plan to remedy any resource deficiencies or management shortcomings that may be identified and steer the work programme back on course. If you are to achieve your objectives despite problems and delays, you may need to require the consultants to put more resources into the work. Whether this is at their own expense as a means of recovering lost ground, or whether you are prepared to meet part or all of the additional costs, is a point that has to be judged against the circumstances of the problem.

- Learn from the experience by analysing what went wrong. Were the key factors recognized by the consultants, or were they beyond their influence or control? If the consultants were aware that things were going wrong, what action did they take and why was it unsuccessful? Was there more that you could have done to avoid the problem? What should you do better next time?

If you are concerned about some aspect of the work, try to clarify the issue as soon as possible by talking to the consultants, but approach them in a constructive rather than confrontational manner. You may have misunderstood what they are trying to do, and a simple explanation may be able to reassure you or a small change in procedure may be enough to sort things out.

The consultants may well come to you to ascertain your views on a particular issue or to get a feel for your reaction to the way the work is turning out. Do not assume that they ought to know what to do without having to ask you, or that because they are asking questions about the work they must be struggling helplessly. They are doing the right thing by trying to avoid wasting time and resources. You should respond to them promptly and honestly.

Be equally prompt and direct when you are convinced there is a real problem. The key is being upfront early on! If there is a member of the team you find useless or impossible to work with, don't feel shy about asking for that person's removal. And certainly don't let your discontent simmer on until it boils up into a crisis. It is in everyone's interests to address the problem quickly and work out a plan to improve the situation in a spirit of cooperation not recrimination.

If there are serious issues to be resolved, it is essential to approach the consultants at the right management level. Consultants do make mistakes; they can give incorrect advice; and they may be guilty of committing bafflingly simple errors – particularly when they are working under pressure; but they can sometimes be stubbornly reluctant to admit that they have gone about things incorrectly. You need to speak to someone in their organization who has no reason to be personally defensive about the work, who has the authority to follow up the substance of your complaint, and who recognizes the strategic importance of quality management to the firm's reputation. And you should make clear what you want the person to do to redress the situation.

Determining what action is needed calls for detailed analysis of the work programme and the relationships and dependencies between its component tasks. This should be undertaken in discussion with the consultants to define the critical path through the work and then identify the additional resources and (in the case of a time-based contract) the additional costs that will be required if the contract is to be completed on time or with the minimum delay.

The level of additional costs is a matter that will have to be negotiated with the consultants. You may want them to reduce their potential charges in compensation for the delay that you have been caused. If a task or activity looks as if it will take longer to complete than was initially estimated, you need to consider ways of getting back on schedule by shortening the time taken to complete other tasks or performing tasks in parallel.

Where time-based contracts are concerned, you have four basic options:

- To make extra funds or extra time available that will allow the work programme to be completed in line with the existing specification. Are you sure just how much more money you will need and where this will come from? And if time is the key factor, can you afford to put back the completion date?

- To cut the work programme down to match your existing funds, for example by leaving out peripheral tasks. Will you still achieve your key objectives?

- To let the consultants carry on until funds run out. How much has been achieved so far, and would terminating the contract cost more?

- To terminate the contract. What will be the implications of not having the work completed?

Despite your best efforts, things may go from bad to worse. The consultants may ignore the concerns you expressed to them, or fail to comply with the terms of their contract, or the working relationship may deteriorate into continual friction. The best course is to bring the contract to an end as soon as you sense that it has broken down irretrievably. It is easier to do that if you have a written contract that defines the circumstances in which it can be terminated (Chapter 6). If the relevant professional body has a complaints procedure, you may also want to invoke that.

Unless the grounds on which you have had to terminate the contract have exposed you to a significant financial loss, it is advisable to avoid legal action and instead use such arbitration or mediation services as may be available. Again, provisions for arbitration may be defined in the terms of the contract.

Good contract management goes much further than ensuring that the agreed terms of the contract are being met – this is a vital step, but only the first of many. No matter what the scope of the contract, there will always be some tensions between the different perspectives of customer and provider. Contract management is about resolving or easing such tensions to build a relationship with the provider based on mutual understanding, trust, open communications and benefits to both customer and provider – a 'win/win' relationship.

Increasingly, public sector organizations are moving away from traditional formal methods of contract management (which tended to keep the provider at arm's length and can become adversarial) and towards building constructive relationships with providers. The management of such a contract, in which the specification may have been for a relationship rather than a particular service, requires a range of 'soft' skills in both the customer and the provider.

A key concept is the relationship that is documented in the contract, not just the mechanics of administering the contract. Agreements, models and processes form a useful starting point for assessing whether the contract is underperforming, but communication, trust, flexibility and diplomacy are the key means through which it can be brought back into line. Adversarial approaches will only increase the distance between customer and provider.

(Source: *Contract Management Guidelines*, Successful Delivery Toolkit, Office of Government Commerce, October 2003)

HANDLING CONTRACT VARIATIONS

If your work specification was carefully thought out and prepared on the basis of accurate information, it is unlikely that the overall scope of the services required from consultants will need to change, though you may have reason to review the details of the work. Over a long-term contract, you may find it necessary to reorient the initial programme of work, perhaps in response to evolving business objectives, emerging issues or new information.

Where changes initiated by you require consultants to do more work than was defined in their contract, you are responsible for paying for the additional work. The point is particularly important in the context of a fixed price contract, which generally allows little or no margin in its cost calculations. Discuss and explain any requirements for change on your part. You must avoid what consultants call 'scope creep' – introducing additional work requirements while expecting consultants to keep to the same fixed price.

There is a counterpart on the consultants' side to scope creep. It principally affects time-based contracts and is the practice of consultants persuading clients to give them more work (ie more fee-earning time) as an extension of an existing assignment. You may be happy to do that if you are sure the additional work will also bring you added value; but if you are at all uncertain, it is advisable to think coolly and objectively about your work requirements and the way they can best be met.

If it is the consultants who are proposing a change in the scope of a fixed price contract, you should ask them to provide a technical and financial justification for the change, and you will need to check back to the contract to judge whether or not what they have in mind can reasonably be interpreted as falling within its terms. A change that is intended to help them overcome difficulties in fulfilling the terms of the contract should be viewed as representing a standard contractor's risk and should warrant no additional payment.

Normally you will need to negotiate with consultants the cost of a contract variation. Ensure that whatever is decided is confirmed in writing, and make it clear that the letter of confirmation will become an integral part of the contract (Figure 7.1).

Dear ....

Contract W123: Modification to contract for consultancy services

We acknowledge receipt of your letter dated .... requesting an amendment to the total of reimbursable expenses indicated in the above-mentioned contract.

After careful consideration we confirm our approval of the following modification:

Reimbursable expenses

Original Total   £35,000
New Total   £55,000 (fifty-five thousand pounds sterling)

This side letter will be annexed to the contract file and will become an integral part of the contract.

Yours sincerely

Figure 7.1 _Example of a side letter modifying a contract_

Dealing with deliverables

When preparing the work specification (Chapter 4), you should have identified the deliverables to be produced by consultants. As noted in Chapter 6, these requirements should form part of the contract for the work. In many areas of consultancy the principal deliverables are reports documenting the results of the consultants' work, often as a narrative that proceeds from the diagnosis of a problem and technical analyses of a situation to proposals for change and recommendations for action.

Documentation may take many other forms, from designs, drawings, graphics, maps and plans to publicity and media material, CDs, DVDs and Web site content. There is a limitless range of other items and services that are common deliverables of consultancy contracts – from training design and delivery, systems procurement advice and market research to quality management systems, contract research programmes and financial policy advice.

Points to check as deliverables come in

- Is the item or service what you expected and has it been delivered on time? If not, what is the reason?

- Does it conform with the requirements defined in the work specification and the contract?

- If the deliverable is a report:

  - Is the information it contains accurate?

  - Is the information sufficient to meet your needs?

  - If you want to use the report to gain funding or support for a business objective, does it make a sound and convincing case?

  - Is information missing?

  - Are there gaps in the logic or the narrative?

  - Do you understand what it says, or are there points that need further explanation?

  - Is it easy to see what the key findings and results are?

Ask consultants to produce summaries of key reports. This is particularly important in contexts where you need to give managers and other decision makers an immediate and sharply focused view of salient points. A summary may be included within the body of the report, but it may also be useful to have it printed as a separate document that can be circulated more widely and cost-effectively than the report itself.

The final output or deliverable of an assignment is often a report. As part of the guidance in Chapter 5, you are advised to indicate in the work specification and the contract that the final deliverable will have to be approved or agreed by you. This is in part to allow you to review it, discuss the findings with business colleagues, correct any factual inaccuracies and request amendments on points that may conflict with cultural or business sensitivities, particularly if the document will carry your name; and in part to avoid a situation in which consultants may claim that the amendment of their draft final report is chargeable as an additional item of work over and above the tasks identified in the work specification. So it is important to stipulate that you will require to see and approve the final report in advance of its formal submission.

You should also insist on seeing drafts of any reports or other documents that are intended for the public to read, for example as part of a consultation exercise or a community involvement programme. Reports can travel far more widely than you may imagine, and communications skills may not be among the consultants' strongest credentials. They may not always give due thought either to the need to say things in language that the public can understand, or to the possibility that what they write may be misinterpreted. If you have management responsibility for a consultancy assignment, you will not wish to neglect the personal and professional risks that attach to ineptly phrased reports.

It is useful to make the same requirement with a report that marks the completion of a stage in a consultancy assignment. Normally the report will need to be reviewed and approved before work starts on the next stage. If consultants are able to outline their findings in advance, you can avoid them having to stop work while awaiting the outcome of your review: there are likely to be aspects of the work that can continue during the review period and bridge the transition into the next stage.

> Quite commonly the final deliverable takes the form of a presentation to interests such as committee members, directors, staff, stakeholders, community groups and so forth, or a workshop at which findings are explained and their implications debated.

Case Study

A travel company that specialized in outdoor pursuit and adventure holidays engaged a shopping research consultancy to update its information base on national and regional trends in online shopping for travel services. A team of research consultants was mobilized to undertake a four-month study of consumer demographics, attitudes and expectations, focusing on trends in metropolitan regions.

The team leader was recruited by the consultancy specifically to coordinate the research: it was only the second assignment that he had managed. A team meeting set up to launch the work and discuss the research programme began inauspiciously with cynical observations from the team leader, who joked about supplying the client with made-up survey data, on the basis that it would take anyone at least six months to discover that the data were fake, by which time the consultancy and the team would have been paid their fees. He also cast doubt on the technical abilities of the partner handling the contract, which led one team member to ask him if he had ever been on a team-building course.

Problems became apparent in the first weeks of the contract. The team leader just did not communicate. The researchers had expected to receive a work plan, method statement and schedule of deliverables, setting out the programme they were supposed to work to. They received nothing except a set of instructions about how the consultancy wanted them to format their reports. For guidance on research methods and procedures, they had to rely on a sketchy description of work requirements prepared by the client. No progress meetings were held, and they seldom saw the team leader, let alone the client. As a result, team members each went about the research in different ways, some more purposefully and competently than others. To make things worse, one researcher turned out to suffer from psychological problems that virtually wrote him off as a team member.

The client's first intervention came two months into the contract: why had the company not been told how the research findings were shaping up, and what exactly had the team been doing? The consultancy reviewed the situation and, in an attempt to give an impression of progress, decided to concentrate on producing an interim report highlighting the fieldwork and desk research undertaken by the two most experienced team members.

This failed to appease the client. In a tense and embarrassing meeting, the research team – minus its leader, who had been taken off the assignment – was reproached for lacking effort, professionalism and direction. The consultancy's senior partner undertook to manage personally the completion of the work at his firm's own expense. Four weeks after the work had been scheduled for completion, the team delivered a report of sorts, but the travel company had a change of strategy in the meantime and never put the research to use.

WHEN THE ASSIGNMENT IS COMPLETED

Obtain a signed and dated final account statement from the consultants. Your organization may require the work to be signed off as completed satisfactorily before a final payment is made. Figure 7.2 shows a simple form of close-out report that provides an opportunity for comments on performance and delivery as well as recording contract data. Figure 7.3 lists the contents of a close-out report used by companies within a large industrial group.

Many consultants will seek feedback soon after an assignment has been completed. They may simply phone or e-mail you for comments or ask you to complete a questionnaire indicating the extent to which their work fulfilled your objectives, whether there were aspects of their performance with which you were particularly pleased or unhappy, and whether you would raise any objection to their citing you as a reference. It is in your interest to be frank and straightforward in your assessment. If the consultants were disappointing in some respect or the results of their work were not as effective in practical terms as you had hoped, it is important to tell them so that they can try to improve their approach.

If the work has gone well – and despite all the talk about problems in this chapter, consultancy assignments often do yield good results – make a point of writing to the consultants to thank them for their efforts, and perhaps indicating your willingness to have your name used in references. It is surprising how many clients regard the payment of an invoice as a sufficient expression of appreciation!

Title of contract		Reference number	
Contract value	Date of contract signature		
Contract amendment(s) and date(s)	Financial period		
Name(s) of consultant(s)			
Key objectives of contract			
Summary description of scope of work			
Scheduled start date	Adhered to? ☐ Yes ☐ No	Observations	
Scheduled completion date	Adhered to? ☐ Yes ☐ No		
Interim milestones	Reached on time? ☐ Yes ☐ No		
Assessment of consultant(s)	Scale: 1 wholly unsatisfactory 2 mostly unsatisfactory 3 acceptable 4 mostly satisfactory 5 wholly satisfactory		
	Score 1–5	Observations	
Technical performance of contract			
Cost control Planned costs .... Actual costs			
Delivery of outputs			
Effort and commitment			
Working relationship			
Quality of consultant management			
Overall assessment			
Has the work achieved its objectives?	☐ Yes ☐ No		
Has the work been completed to your satisfaction?	☐ Yes ☐ No		
Do you recommend future use of the consultant(s)?	☐ Yes ☐ No		

The work undertaken by .... in the above contract is/is not signed off as satisfactorily completed. *Delete as appropriate.*

Signed .... Post ....

Dated ....

Figure 7.2 *Example of a close-out form*

Checklist for Close-out Report

☐ Introduction: a brief description of the objectives of the consultancy.

☐ Technical and business justification for the consultancy.

☐ Statement of requirements, including scope of work (tasks and activities), deliverables and timescale.

☐ Change register: a summary of any significant change that affected the consultancy delivery.

☐ Expand on specific areas of change that had a critical effect on the work.

☐ Performance of consultants, sub-consultants, other specialists and suppliers and the Business Team.

☐ Include a project organization chart.

☐ Comment on the effectiveness of this organizational structure with regard to communication channels and reporting relationships.

☐ State your view as to whether the mobilized resources were sufficient to carry out the work in an effective manner.

☐ Show project milestones and key activities in bar chart format.

☐ Explain planned original versus actual achievement, with any variances.

☐ Cost summary: include 'S' curves showing planned original versus actual costs. Provide an overall cost analysis to show original and final budgets plus major areas of expenditure and any variations.

☐ Identify any problems related to compliance with the specification and technical interfaces.

☐ Comments and recommendations: include a summary of strengths, weaknesses, recommendations, lessons learnt by the Business Team, and scope for further improvement.

Hard copies of the completed report are to be distributed to the following: Business Client, Task Managers, Programme Manager and the project file.

Figure 7.3 _Example of a close-out report structure_

8

How does the public sector go about procurement?

Though the preceding chapters are addressed largely to individuals and businesses in the private sector, much of their content will be relevant also to public sector organizations. There are broad similarities in the approaches that characterize the procurement of consultancy services in each sector – including an emphasis on obtaining good value for money, achieving efficient performance and delivery and building constructive relationships. But public sector authorities have less flexibility in the way they select consultants and award contracts, and they are generally required to operate within a procedural environment that is defined by legislation.

These differences are the subject of this chapter. The discussion relates principally to public sector organizations in the UK and other EU member states, ie central government, regional and local authorities, utilities and other bodies governed by public law. Public sector procurement in the United States, Canada and Australia has points in common with practice in the EU, but the procedural requirements of federal and state agencies are too varied to allow their inclusion in this brief survey.

Research undertaken in 2000 for the former UK Department for Transport, Local Government and the Regions (DTLR) by its Local and Regional Government Research Unit offers an indication of the extent to which local authorities in England use consultants. Some 70 per cent of the authorities surveyed used consultants and expected to continue to engage their services over the long term. Almost 80 per cent used consultants to help draw up work specifications for service contracts.

PROCUREMENT RULES AND REGULATIONS

Public sector organizations in EU member states are required in law to seek competitive tenders for all except small and relatively low-value contracts. The requirement stems from European Commission directives that are intended: 1) to secure open and fair competition with equal access to contract opportunities and equal and non-discriminatory treatment for all EU suppliers; and 2) to establish transparent and auditable contracting procedures so that public money is spent in a way that achieves the best value for taxpayers.

During 2002 and 2003 a new EC procurement directive was developed, consolidating the existing public works, services and supplies directives into a single text. The broad aim of the new directive is to simplify and coordinate procedures for the award of public contracts, updating them to reflect the advent of new technologies such as e-communication, removing elements of ambiguity and rigidity and increasing the transparency of contract award procedures. The directive introduces a new procedure termed 'competitive dialogue', which can be used in awarding contracts for complex projects and is intended to help public authorities identify the best means of meeting their requirements through negotiation and the progressive refinement of technical solutions.

The public sector directive is accompanied by another new directive that consolidates the rules applying to utilities, defined as entities operating in the water, energy, transport and telecommunications sectors. Utilities are required to comply with procurement rules that differ in points of detail from those applying to other public bodies.

The EC directives are put into practice at a member state level through regulations and other forms of legislation. New regulations implementing the consolidated directives are likely to come into force by the end of 2004. In the meantime the existing regulations apply.

Public sector contracting for services and consultancy in the UK is governed principally by the following regulations:

- The Public Services Contracts Regulations 1993;

- The Public Contracts (Works, Services and Supply) (Amendment) Regulations 2000;

- The Utilities Contracts Regulations 1996;

- The Utilities Contracts (Amendment) Regulations 2001;

- The Public Contracts (Works, Services and Supply) and Utilities Contracts (Amendment) Regulations 2003. These largely implement an EC directive on the use of standard forms for contract notices as part of the introduction of electronic procurement.

Within this procurement framework, public authorities in the UK are able to apply their own detailed procedures for tendering and contract award on the basis of standing orders, provided these do not infringe EC rules or the requirements of UK legislation and government accounting principles.

The detailed application of the procurement rules is a complex matter, and it is likely to remain complex after the new consolidated procedures come into effect. There are circumstances that give rise to exemptions and exceptions from the general rules, and aspects of the existing directives are open to differing interpretations. It is essential for clients in the public sector to be adequately informed about the mechanics of the procurement regime so as not to find themselves taking the wrong course of action.

The Office of Government Commerce (OGC) is a source of authoritative guidance on the EC procurement rules and related topics. The texts of existing UK contracts regulations and EC directives can be downloaded from its site (www.ogc.gov.uk), which has a link to the EC site. As part of its task of promoting greater efficiency in public sector procurement and project delivery, OGC produces a flow of best practice advice for public authorities in the UK. Key documents include:

- _Improving the Efficiency and Effectiveness of Procurement to Achieve Faster Delivery_ (published in June 2003);

- _Forming Partnering Relationships with the Private Sector_ (December 2002);

- *Risk Allocation in Long-Term Contracts* (December 2002);

- *Contract Management Guidelines* (November 2002);

- *Value for Money Evaluation in Major Service Procurements* (March 2002).

OGC also offers briefing notes for public authorities on project management, risk management and successful delivery skills. Its *Successful Delivery Toolkit* includes a series of workbooks and other guidance on best practice in procurement and contract management, including business justification, procurement strategy, investment decisions and effective partnering. The OGC Gateway process, developed as a means of reviewing delivery programmes and procurement projects in central government at key decision points in their life cycle, is now being extended to local authorities. At the time of writing (April 2004) the reviews are on a voluntary basis, undertaken by the Public Private Partnerships Programme (4ps), which provides support for local authorities to help improve their procurement capabilities.

This emphasis on efficient management, performance and delivery is normally reflected in the work specifications for high-value public sector contracts by a requirement to provide plans for progress measurement, performance monitoring, quality control and the management of risk and change. The DTLR research found that virtually all local authorities in England measured the performance of their external contractors.

THE PROCUREMENT PROCESS

The procurement rules cover the entire process of contracting from the advertisement of contract opportunities and publication of contract notices to pre-qualification, tendering procedures, tender evaluation and contract award. The contract value thresholds at which the rules apply are set out in Figure 8.1. Figure 8.2 indicates the principal actions that might be taken by a public sector authority and a consultant respectively in a typical procurement process for consultancy services. The process is shown as far as, but does not include, the stage of contract negotiation.

All contracts for which public authorities invite tenders are announced through a contract notice in Supplement S of the *Official Journal of the European Communities (OJS)*. The supplement is updated daily and

---

Financial thresholds

Specific rules apply to contracts with values at or exceeding financial thresholds set out in the public procurement regulations; contracts with lower values are subject to less stringent requirements. The regulations include formulae for calculating values for a series of contracts and for framework agreements.

In January 2004 new threshold values came into effect, which will remain unchanged for two years in the case of EU member states outside the single currency. The sterling values of these thresholds are calculated on the basis of exchange rates between sterling, euros and special drawing rights (a currency unit devised by the IMF).

Contracts with values at or above the following sterling amounts, net of VAT, are subject to the procurement rules, with certain exceptions that chiefly affect categories of research and development and telecommunications services.

	Threshold
Services contracts – central government	£99,695
Services contracts – other public sector authorities	£153,376
Services contracts – public sector small lots	£51,785
Utilities services contracts – water, electricity, urban transport, airports and ports sectors	£306,753
Utilities services contracts – oil, gas, coal and railway sectors	£258,923
Utilities services contracts – telecommunications	£388,385

(Source: Office of Government Commerce)

Figure 8.1 *Public sector procurement: contract value thresholds*

available online at http://ted.publications.eu.int. Tender opportunities that are part of EC-funded programmes may be notified also through Internet announcements on programme Web sites. Authorities may use the *OJS* also to publicize contracts that are not subject to notification requirements. Decisions on how and where to advertise such contracts are left to the discretion of authorities: generally, notices may be placed in the national, regional and local press and in technical and trade publications.

The points of information that have to feature in the contract notice include:

Local authority	Consultant
Planning and preparation	
Consultation and market testing to ensure that procurement strategy and contracting practices are conducive to securing an effective competitive response	**Market analyses and business strategy** **Focus on target sectors** **Market intelligence for contract opportunities** **Researching the client** **Contacts with client managers**
Project definition and design, including **drafting of work specification**	
Decision to adopt the **restricted procedure**	
Determination of **contract award criteria, weightings** and **quality:price ratio** (see Chapter 5)	
Appointment of **assessment and selection panel**	
Review of **supplier database**, registration and pre-qualification information	
Notification and pre-qualification	
Initial advertisement and contract notice, inviting expressions of interest	**Preparation and submission of expression of interest**
First stage of selection: assessment panel filters expressions of interest and, if necessary, reduces list to a manageable total for second stage of selection	
Second stage of selection: a more detailed assessment of prospective bidders, possibly including interviews and visits	
Definition of **shortlist** – say, five selected bidders	
Tendering	
Finalization of work specification	
Issue of **proposal invitations and accompanying documentation**	**Acknowledgement of invitation** **Decision to bid** **Confirmation of intention to submit a proposal**

Figure 8.2 *Steps in a typical local authority procurement process for consultancy*

Decisions on **evaluation approach**	**Analysis of work specification** **Preparation of proposal**
Arrangements for dealing with **clarification requests**	**Request for clarification**
Formal site visits or briefings, if appropriate	**Briefing or meeting with client, if appropriate**
Receipt of proposals	**Submission of proposal**
Evaluation	
Formal **tender opening** and **checks for compliance**	
Proposal evaluation – quality and price	
Arrangements for **presentations** by lead contenders	
Preparation of format and key questions for presentations	**Preparation of presentation**
Assessment of presentations	**Delivery of presentation**
Further clarification of contract issues, if appropriate	Further clarification of contract issues, if appropriate
Selection of the most economically advantageous tender	
Contract award	
Notification to successful bidder, including any **conditions** to be discussed at contract negotiation stage	
Notification to unsuccessful bidders, including placing a reserve or hold on the bidder ranked second in case negotiations with the first-ranked bidder fail	

Figure 8.2 *continued*

- the purpose and scope of the contract;
- legal, economic and technical conditions for participation;
- whether a fee has to be paid to obtain contract documents or work specifications;

- whether provision of a service is restricted to a particular profession;

- the type of procedure to be followed in awarding the contract;

- the criteria to be applied in evaluating tenders, stated so far as possible in descending order of importance;

- the time limits for the receipt of tenders or requests to participate;

- the language or languages in which tenders or requests to participate can be prepared.

Contract award procedures

Authorities have a choice of four types of contract award procedure:

- **Open procedure.** Any consultant or service provider may submit a tender in response to the contract notice. This procedure can have disadvantages for authorities in terms of the time and resources needed to process what might turn out to be an inordinate number of bids, and may lead consultants to question the likely quality and thoroughness of the tender evaluation. On the other hand, it can provide an opportunity for authorities to learn about sources of expertise and solutions that they might not have considered.

- **Restricted procedure.** Consultants have first to submit an expression of interest or a request to be selected as a candidate for tendering through pre-qualification (Chapter 5). The authority then invites tenders from the pre-qualified candidates. In an urgent and exceptional situation, this process may be accelerated: the reasons justifying acceleration must be explained in the contract notice.

- **Negotiated procedure.** A contracting authority may go directly to one or more consultants or service providers and negotiate with them the terms of a contract. This type of procedure is used only in relatively exceptional cases, for example when the nature of the services makes it unfeasible to apply either the open or restricted procedure, or when the services and their inherent risks do not allow prior overall pricing.

- **Competitive dialogue.** Noted earlier in the chapter, this is a development of the negotiated procedure. An authority may pursue a process of dialogue with selected tenderers through successive rounds of negotiation until it has identified the solution most likely to satisfy its needs. The participants are then asked to submit their final tenders on the basis of that solution. The contract is awarded to the participant judged to have submitted the tender that is the most economically advantageous, as defined below.

Most contracts with values that make them subject to the public procurement rules are awarded under the restricted procedure. The sequence of activities shown in Figure 8.2 illustrates this procedure.

The rules for the open and restricted procedures do not forbid contracting authorities from discussing forthcoming opportunities with potential bidders and encouraging them to express interest, provided there is no element of discrimination in these contacts. Once the tendering process starts, the scope for discussion becomes much narrower so as to ensure that all bidders are treated fairly and even-handedly. Explaining matters of fact or process is fine – and the procurement rules define a formal scheme for responding to requests for clarification in a way that avoids any suggestion of treating one bidder more favourably than another. But discussing issues related to price, personnel or the technical content of a tender is unacceptable under the existing rules.

Pre-qualification

Pre-qualification for public contracts has to be based on objective and non-discriminatory criteria that relate to the legal situation of bidders and their technical, economic and financial capacity. Technical capacity is judged on the basis of resources, quality standards and past perform-ance, including references from other clients. So far as financial status is concerned, clients may look for evidence that a bidder is considered likely to remain in business over and beyond the lifetime of the contract. To secure an adequate degree of competition, the shortlist resulting from the pre-qualification process will normally have a minimum of five names and perhaps as many as seven or eight. Bidders are entitled to receive an explanation of the reasons for their failure to pre-qualify.

Output-based specifications

In almost all fields of public sector procurement, bidders will be respond-ing to 'output-based' specifications. Put simply, an output-based specification is a document that defines the authority's needs in terms of the results the work is intended to produce, the services that are to be delivered or the functions that are to be performed, without getting into the detail of how those results, services or functions might be achieved. So far as possible, it steers clear of prescribing required solutions or methods and gives bidders the flexibility to devise new and innovative approaches.

The specification may state the minimum services or functions that are to be provided. It may also draw a distinction between primary or mandatory output requirements that the contracting authority regards as critically important for the successful performance of the work, and secondary or desirable output requirements that offer benefits but are not considered essential. In developing a specification, the authority will normally aim to identify at the start the changes in requirements that are likely to emerge during the course of the work, particularly if the specification relates to a long-term service contract: these changes and the costs that they are expected to entail will form an integral part of the agreement between the authority and the successful bidder.

Figure 8.3 outlines the structure of a typical output-based specification. The example is derived from a model developed within the UK National Health Service for the procurement of IT services and equipment, but its broad outlines are characteristic of public sector procurement in general. It has been edited here to remove structural features that are appropriate only for large-scale contracts.

Tender evaluation and contract award

Public sector contracts are awarded on the basis of either the lowest price or the tender that is the most economically advantageous for the contracting authority. In services procurement, lowest price is normally used as the sole criterion only in awarding low-value and relatively low-risk contracts. For other contracts, authorities generally prefer the concept of the most economically advantageous tender, which means the tender that offers the best value for money, taking account of technical merit and quality as well as price and cost-effectiveness.

Value for money is defined by the Office of Government Commerce as the optimum combination of whole-life costs and quality to meet the customer's requirements. So far as services and consultancy are concerned, the definition can be rephrased as 'meeting the user's requirements with the best quality of service at the right price'.

Section	Content
1 Introduction	Description of the client organization
	Purpose, content and scope of the specification: what is included and excluded
	Disclaimers, caveats, etc
	Confidentiality of content
2 Background	Summary of business strategy and procurement process
	Client policies, structures and functions relevant to the proposed contract
	Outline of organization, staffing, stakeholders, information flows and so forth
	Relevant history and proposed developments
3 Objectives	Business and technical objectives of the proposed contract
	Summary of expected outcomes and benefits from the investment
	Summary of the scope of the procurement, including core elements, optional extensions and exclusions
4 Core requirements	Definition of the client's core requirements Specification of system-related outputs (including application functionality if appropriate):
	– nature: ie high level functionality – volumetrics: eg frequency, volume – quality attributes: eg format, reliability, accuracy and response times
	Specification of primary and secondary output requirements
	Specification of services inputs (ie outputs from the client to the contractor)
	Requirements related to migration, implementation and start-up of new facilities or services
	Requirements related to the end-of-contract period and possible transition to a new service/supplier
	Items on which contractors are required to provide detailed information - for example, their approach to specific aspects of the contract

Figure 8.3 _Structure of a typical output-based specification_

Section		Content
5	Additional and optional services and/or activities	Requirements for additional services and activities
		Optional additions to the scope of the contract
		Opportunities for contract variation
6	Management of contract	Requirements for service management, quality management and monitoring, management information, client/customer liaison, contract review arrangements and so forth
7	Constraints	Constraints to be observed in the solutions proposed: for example – conformity with standards, interfacing with other systems, interaction with other business activities, adaptability of existing processes, timing considerations and so forth
8	Risk management	Inventory of risks related to the contract
		Client view on risk ownership and allocation
		Requirement for contractors to complete risk ownership tables and indicate proposed contractual mechanisms for risk transfer and management
9	Procurement process	Procurement timetable and procedures
		Evaluation methods and criteria
		Implementation timetable
10	Required content of contractor's response	Instructions on format and structure of proposals
		Form of tender and related documentation
		Compliance criteria
		Requirements for: – detailed response to the content of the specification – submission of financial information – details of options or alternative proposals – description of approach to service provision (including project management, plans, timetable, organization and staffing and related items) – client references
11	Annexes	Business plans
		Strategy documents
		Statistical material and so forth

Figure 8.3 *continued*

The procurement regulations give examples of criteria that may be applied to identify the most economically advantageous tender – including quality, technical merit, aesthetic and functional characteristics, delivery date or period for completion, running costs, long-term cost-effectiveness and so forth, as well as price. But an authority is able to make its own choice of criteria to suit the particular requirements of a contract, provided the criteria used: 1) permit objective assessment; 2) are free from bias or discrimination; 3) are related to the essential features of the contract in question; and 4) generate an economic advantage for the contracting authority.

Authorities normally undertake a compliance check at the start of the evaluation to confirm that all the information requested from consultants is contained in the proposal and set out in the required format. The documentation submitted by consultants may be required to include a collusive tendering certificate, in which bidders declare that they have not come to an understanding with another person to fix or adjust the amount of the tender, and undertake among other matters not to disclose the amount of the tender to any unauthorized person before the contract is awarded or to arrange that another person should either not put in a tender or should pitch a tender at a certain price.

Because the process that leads to identification of the most economically advantageous tender needs to be auditable and objective, most public sector authorities employ a form of marking scheme in which each bid is scored against the defined criteria, which are weighted to reflect their degree of priority. The bids are then ranked in the order of their total scores. Either the bid with the highest score is selected as the winning bid, or – if the evaluation is in two parts, the first concerned with technical merit and the second with price – those bids with total scores at or above a pre-set threshold (say 65 or 70 points out of a maximum 100) go forward to a financial evaluation before being given a final rank on the basis of their combined and weighted technical and financial scores. This final rank identifies the most economically advantageous tender.

The relative weight given to the technical and financial scores in this calculation (the quality:price ratio) may follow a set formula (eg 70 per cent quality, 30 per cent price) or it may be decided on a case-by-case basis. As a general principle, the more a contract for services demands complex analytical work or innovative thinking, the greater the weight attached to quality in the bid evaluation: so, for example, the quality:price ratio for a strategic planning contract or a feasibility study might be set at 80:20. These values are likely to be reversed for what may be considered routine, straightforward work or repeat projects, where the emphasis will be predominantly on price.

The structure of the marking scheme will be conditioned by the nature of the contract. In cases where the standard of contract performance appears likely to be determined by the calibre of the key people undertaking the work, 50 to 60 per cent of the technical evaluation marks may be awarded in respect of personnel, while the proposed methodology may carry 30 to 40 per cent and the qualifications and experience of the consultants 10 per cent. If the bid names a team leader or project manager, this individual's competence, suitability and experience can have a critical bearing on the marks awarded for personnel. Methodology may have more importance in the marking where the contract involves intricate processes of technical analysis.

Authorities may base the financial evaluation on a comparison of total bid prices, unit prices (for example, fees and direct costs divided by the number of staff/days or staff/months) or the overall costs of the required services over the life of the contract (whole-life costs). Various formulas may be applied in scoring price. For example, where a quality:price ratio of 70:30 is used, the lowest-priced bid may automatically be awarded the full 30 points available and the other bids marked by dividing their prices into the lowest price and multiplying the result of the division by 30; or the mean price of, say, the three lowest-priced bids may be given a value of 30 points, and one point may then be deducted from the score of each bidder for each percentage point above the mean, while one point is added to the score of each bidder for each percentage point below the mean.

For large-scale and high-value contracts, the client may undertake tender evaluation in two stages. The first stage uses the process of technical and financial evaluation described here to identify, say, two or three shortlisted bidders who are asked in the second stage to refine their bids and develop further their proposed solutions to the client's requirements. Commercial negotiations may start during this second stage. The shortlisted bidders will be evaluated on their final responses and the client will then select a preferred bidder for detailed negotiations.

The evaluation process may include interviews and presentations. Before formally awarding a contract, clients may wish to refer their selection decision to an independent expert for endorsement, for example on the value-for-money aspects of a bid.

In summary, what differentiates public sector procurement from practice in the private sector is not so much the approach followed by public authorities as the legal requirement to act within a defined procedural framework. After all, most of us recognize that if we are uncertain about whom to engage it makes sense to seek competitive bids, that we are more likely to achieve good results from the tendering process if we treat all tenderers fairly, and that what really counts is getting the best value for money. The concept of the most economically advantageous tender is not one that is foreign to the private sector. Business clients too appreciate that in working with consultants they get what they pay for, and that people who offer services at rates cut to the bone may be offering also low quality, poor performance and minimal standards of professionalism.

BEST VALUE AND PARTNERING

There are two further principles that may influence the performance of public sector service contracts – best value and partnering. The Local Government Act 1999 introduced a duty on every public authority to undertake best value reviews of its services. These reviews ask several basic questions:

- Are the authority's services to the community yielding the best value for money?

- How are they valued by the taxpayer?

- Should those services be provided at all?

- If they should, is there a better way to provide them?

Best value reviews challenge the authority's activities against the preferences and expectations of service users and stakeholders, and apply the results to develop plans that can address gaps and short-comings and secure a programme of continuous improvement in service delivery. Depending on the nature and scale of a contract, public sector authorities may require service providers and consultants to work within the terms of the best value regime.

Partnering and the development of long-term, collaborative working relationships are discussed in Chapter 9. Half the authorities surveyed in 2000 had adopted partnering as their preferred approach to supplier relationships, principally in sectors such as education, social services, construction, property management, highways and transport, and waste management. Partnering arrangements with public authorities are subject to the EC procurement rules. In the view of the Office of Government Commerce, the benefits of partnering include increased scope for innovation and responsive customer service; a firm and stable basis for long-term planning; more effective risk allocation and management; and a reduced burden of contract administration costs on the public authority.

Detailed information on the commissioning of services by local authorities in the UK is available in a guide published by the Commissioning Joint Committee, a body sponsored by the Chartered Institute of Public Finance and Accountancy (CIPFA). Obtainable on subscription from CIPFA (www.cipfa.org.uk), the guide is distributed principally on CD ROM.

9

How can I get the best value from consultants?

- 'Delivering what we want when we need it.'

- 'Giving us the best possible service for the price we are paying.'

- 'Work we don't regret spending money on.'

- 'Consultants who deliver what they promise.'

- 'Acceptable quality at an affordable cost.'

- 'Reports that we can understand.'

. . . Some of the ways clients express what value means to them. What does it mean to you? It is important to think about this at the outset, when you start to map out your requirements. The work specification that you send to consultants has to give them a clear sense of your perception of value and your expectations about the results they are to deliver.

The quality, cost-effectiveness and performance of the service you receive will figure prominently in any analysis of value. This analysis needs to reflect directly your purpose in approaching consultants (Chapter 1). If you are seeking specialist skills, value may consist principally in the extent to which consultants possess the required expertise and are able to apply it in serving your needs. If your aim is a neutral and dispassionate view, their degree of objectivity and the soundness of their logic will be critical factors. If you are using them to obtain fresh resources, you may view their value as the energy and brainpower they bring to the work.

One factor that your analysis of value ought not to neglect is the practicality and usefulness of the consultants' work. How closely does their advice match your business requirements, and how feasible will it be to put their recommendations or findings into effect? Will the outcome of their work be sustainable by your own people after the consultants have left the scene? Consultants who give positive results on these counts are likely also to demonstrate value in terms of their understanding of your business environment and their ability to deliver a targeted response to your requirements rather than an off-the-shelf solution. In a sense, one can regard the consultants who give value as those who maximize the benefits their work offers clients while minimizing the risks attached to its performance.

SECURING ADDED VALUE

Adding value to a contract is often defined as delivering more outputs or a better quality of service at no extra cost. To achieve this, consultants need to recognize and reinforce the factors that have key importance for a client – whether those factors are the efficient control of budgets and work plans and the successful management of risk, the acquisition of new skills and competencies, or the development of opportunities to gain business advantages and new sources of revenue.

But consultants can add value also through the type of approach they bring to their work – for example, by adapting to changing requirements during the course of a contract and responding with new ideas that benefit its performance and its outcome. Consultancy is or ought to be a questioning and challenging mode of activity. One of the most valuable things consultants can do is to encourage you to ask yourself, for example, why your business goes about its affairs in a particular way, why you take a particular view of this or that issue, and whether there might be a better means of achieving your objectives. Consultants who are knowledgeable about your business environment can yield long-term benefits by helping you unlock new potential and move in new directions. There is a clear parallel here with best value reviews in the public sector, which provoke challenges to existing ways of thinking, a search for better solutions and a drive for continuous improvement in performance.

That is why it is important, when selecting consultants, to look beyond technical ability and management capacity, and to search for the particular quality of insight and vision that differentiates the consultants who are right for you. Their bid will have an extra dimension that shows creativity and innovation allied to a purposeful drive and direction.

For some clients the added value of consultants is measured in terms of the extent to which their presence and intervention make life easier. The consultants they want to use are those who understand what their clients expect and know the right things to do without having to be told, and who are prepared to put an extra effort into the work and go that bit further to ensure a satisfactory result.

VIEWPOINT

'We have used consultants fairly regularly, mainly in fields such as survey design, statistical analysis, management training and marketing. The results have been variable. One factor that makes a big difference is the background of the consultancy firm and the attitudes that its personnel bring to their work. I suppose this can be described as the ethos or culture of the firm.

'I can cite some examples. One group of consultants we used had started life as an internal consultancy unit in a local authority, part of the policy of compulsory competitive tendering in the mid-1990s. They were quite competent technically, and their local authority knowledge was relevant to the particular assignment, but they lacked any real understanding of business. Their output was not as useful as we had hoped. It focused on their technical procedures instead of our commercial priorities. We had the impression that they had thought they could turn themselves into a consultancy overnight, simply by replacing the "Design Department" sign above their door by one that read "Design Associates".

'We were disappointed also by a university group that we contracted to help us with some statistical work. The problem was that they did not seem to be sure what business they were in. Their first priority was not our needs as a client but their own research programmes. We took second place and our work was fitted in when it suited their timetable. We were also unhappy about having research students undertaking aspects of the work that we believed to need analysis at a more senior level. There was no sense of urgency or responsive management on their part. Cynically one might say they had the advantage of being cheap, because they charged at uncommercial rates. But a more professional outfit would have been a better buy.

'Not surprisingly, we have achieved the best results and the best value when we have used firms that started life as consultancies and that have proved themselves through genuine professionalism. The quality of their work is consistently dependable; they have some first-class people; they keep on their toes and care about getting things right. There is a sense that they are putting us first, thinking about our business needs, supporting our objectives and developing perceptive solutions specifically for us. Their professionalism means that we enjoy working with them; they appreciate being valued; and the result is a relationship that we are happy to maintain.'

(Director, train operating company)

CREATING A COLLABORATIVE BUSINESS RELATIONSHIP

A client–consultant relationship that is maintained over the long term, proven through experience and marked by honesty and trust generates value for both parties. To the client it offers a secure and dependable source of advice. For the consultants it means the prospect of continued work, provided results are good and standards remain high. In this type of relationship the consultancy assignment is viewed as a collaborative endeavour between the client's staff and the consultants' personnel. They work as a team to achieve the objectives of the assignment and show an identity of purpose based on their joint interest in making it succeed. The consultants see the work in the same perspective as the client though from an independent professional standpoint.

In recent years, supply chain partnering, which was developed initially as a means of strengthening and integrating supply processes in industry, has found increasing application in the context of consultancy projects and service provision in both the private and public sectors (Chapter 8). Figure 9.1 shows the main stages in a typical partnering process. The key principle is that consultants, subcontractors and specialists are treated as interdependent links in a chain of professional responsibility, aligned within an agreed structure of delivery and acting together as a team to manage the risks inherent in a contract. Specifications are usually non-prescriptive, and consultants and subcontractors are encouraged to add value through innovative solutions. Each link in the chain receives the support of other partners in delivering its contribution, and problems are resolved through a cooperative approach before they can threaten the progress of the work. The team members sign up to the relationship through a partnering agreement, which may be developed into a single partnering contract (Chapter 6).

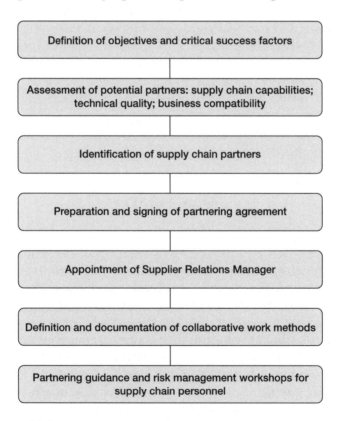

Figure 9.1 _Main stages in a partnering process_

The adage about the weakest link is as true of this type of chain as of any other; and creating a relationship of this kind takes time, patience and long-term commitment – it isn't something that can be constructed to order. But the process has clear advantages for clients engaged in consultancy projects that involve complex supply lines and that rely critically on an efficient and conscientious performance by specialist advisers. By eliminating unnecessary interfaces and reducing the potential for friction and conflict, it can cut costs, add value and ensure that the work is focused accurately on the client's requirements.

Figure 9.2 at the end of this chapter is an edited extract from guidance on partnering produced by the Office of Government Commerce. The guidance was drawn up primarily to assist in the successful development of partnering arrangements with IT service providers.

Outside the field of service provision, relatively few business clients may be able to offer the continuity of work that would justify a long-term partnering relationship with consultants, as distinct from other types of contractor or supplier. Yet the ideas on which partnering is based make good business sense for any organization or individual that has reason to use consultants and advisers. Treating consultancy as a collaborative process, building joint accountability and commitment, seeing consultants as part of the team, viewing the costs of their professional judgement as an investment in minimizing risk – these are principles that will help you get best value from the relationship and make working with consultants really worthwhile.

Case study

The 1960s saw the birth of several UK firms of architects and planning consultants that quickly built up an impressive record both at home and overseas. One feature they had in common was a kind of planetary structure, in which partners and associates orbited round a central star – usually an eminent practitioner – who provided the charisma that attracted commissions and sustained the firm's growth. In the course of time, as their stellar founders came to retire, these firms found it necessary to reshape their structure while seeking to maintain their thrust and momentum.

By the late 1990s one such firm had lost both the brilliance that marked its youth and the reputation it had enjoyed for professional value. In the past, bright young graduates had queued to join the firm and had seen it as an enviable place to develop their careers. Now there was an alarmingly high turnover of staff and a shrinking order book. People in other consultancies shook their heads and talked about the firm seeming to have a death wish.

In 1999 a new generation of partners realized that consultants too might sometimes be in need of consultancy advice. They called in management consultants who had worked with them as associates on a number of projects. The brief was to see how the firm could be given a fresh lease of life and transformed into a faster, smarter and more responsive business.

The management consultants identified three areas where they believed a change of approach was essential. First, the younger members of staff had to be encouraged to feel they had a stake in the firm's future. Thus far they had been offered no involvement in business decisions that affected the way their skills were applied. For a firm that was frequently engaged to run public involvement programmes as part of its planning work, it undertook surprisingly little internal consultation with its own staff. With the help of the management consultants, the firm set up a series of focus teams enlisting the participation of all staff and introduced a bonus and incentive scheme to reward ideas and performance. The focus teams were an immediate success: one young graduate remarked 'Customers vote "yes" or "no" in the marketplace, so we need to vote "yes" or "no" in the workplace.'

Secondly, the consultants designed and helped to launch a new business strategy that they termed 'enhanced quality performance', intended to strengthen professional commitment and deliver services that met or exceeded client expectations. There was nothing new about the thinking behind the strategy, but it was the first time that the firm had made a concerted effort to put quality improvement into practice.

The third area of change saw the firm redefining its target market and searching for new growth sectors, related to the firm's experience but responding to new requirements on the part of clients and offering fresh potential for the skills of its staff. Clues to where the market was heading were there to be discovered by consultants alert to trends and developments in their fields. The firm took on new specialists and formed strategic alliances with other consultancies and research centres.

Over the past year or so staff turnover has dropped appreciably and financial results have improved. Customer satisfaction too has risen: it has some way to go to reach 100 per cent but is on a steady climb. The firm's recent successes have begun to worry its competitors. No one now sees it as destined for an early demise.

Using consultants: 20 pointers to success

- If you decide to use consultants, make sure it's for the right reasons.

- Start with a clear idea of what you want to achieve and a confident view of the benefits you hope to gain from the work.

- If you have staff, win their support and confidence.

- Think your requirements through in detail. Be realistic about the scope of the work, its timescale and the budget that is available.

- Prepare a work specification that communicates clearly your requirements and expectations and is accurately matched to your budget. Time spent at this stage will save you money later.

- Decide what needs to be specified in detail, but let consultants apply their expertise and experience in judging how the work can best be done.

- Identify the resources that you have to put into the work and ensure they are available when needed.

- Consider what can go wrong and how you can prevent problems from developing.

- Take up the consultants' references to find out what they are like to work with.

- The consultants' skills and years of experience have a value that is reflected in their fees. Recognize this when you ask them for a quotation.

- If you go out to tender, make sure the process is fair and transparent. Give bidders full and accurate information.

- Assess tenders in terms of value for money, not necessarily the lowest price.

- When awarding a contract, take account of competence, reliability, the quality of the consultants' response, the degree of business insight that they show and the potential for a constructive working relationship.

- Choose the right form of contract. Make sure its meaning is absolutely clear. If you are drawing up the contract yourself, include all the points needed to ensure a clear statement of responsibilities and a fair allocation of risk. If you are in any doubt, get legal advice.

■ If the consultants have prepared terms of engagement, check that you understand and are happy with every clause. Sign the agreement only if you can accept it in full.

■ Ensure the work is managed in a focused and determined way. Keep track of its progress and check performance.

■ Remember that it is your objectives that must set the pace of work.

■ Maintain an open and transparent dialogue with the consultants.

■ Flag up issues and difficulties as early as possible. If there are problems to be resolved, tackle them at the right level.

■ The key ingredients of success in working with consultants are: first, defining clear and sensible objectives; second, conveying your requirements and priorities efficiently; third, ensuring the consultants share your understanding of professionalism and the importance of businesslike performance; and fourth, sustaining a relationship based on confidence and trust.

Effective partnering

The following guidance is an edited extract from *Effective partnering; an overview for customers and providers*, published in March 2004 by the Office of Government Commerce as part of its Successful Delivery Toolkit.

This guidance is primarily intended for those leading the project and programme teams in the customer and provider organizations. It will also be of interest to everyone who may be involved in a partnering arrangement.

The tone of a **partnering arrangement** differs from a traditional contract and the behaviours of those involved are different too. The management of a partnering arrangement is usually proactive rather than reactive. Both parties work together to identify optimum solutions and to anticipate and resolve problems in a constructive, collaborative way. The arrangement needs to be based on mutual trust and openness, a recognition that the relationship itself is as important as the contract and a conviction that partnering makes good commercial sense for this particular programme.

Modern commercial arrangements should be based on the following principles:

Figure 9.2 *Guidance on partnering*

- a shared understanding of what the desired outcome is and which elements are to be provided by each party;

- focus on benefits – not just on time and cost;

- shared understanding of which party is managing particular elements of risk;

- (for long term contracts) ability to cope with changing customer requirements and technology developments;

- capability of implementing efficient and effective procurement.

Partnering extends these principles. For the customer organization, a good partnering arrangement offers the benefits of proactive risk allocation, technical innovation, flexibility and improved value for money. For the service provider, the benefits include more involvement in management decisions, greater freedom to suggest innovative solutions, and better insight into the customer's business (as well as commercial gain). For both parties, shared business objectives and a collaborative approach to achieving them mean that the partnering approach offers significant strategic benefits. Partnering is about strength through collaboration. Building and maintaining a partnering arrangement will take much more effort and time than a traditional approach, not least because new attitudes and behaviours may have to be learned – and old ones unlearned.

When should partnering be used?
Partnering is not appropriate in every situation. It is a long term relationship, usually over five years and often much longer, where customers and providers adopt long term rather than short term views. Partnering may be suitable where there is a need for:

- business change, especially where innovation is required and/or the future is uncertain;

- using new methods of service delivery (such as providing services online);

- flexibility in constructing teams, involving specialist skills or scarce resources;

- outsourcing business processes or services, perhaps to allow customer staff to concentrate on core areas.

Partnering is unlikely to be suitable for:

- short term requirements where there will not be time for the provider to recover initial investment costs;

Figure 9.2 *continued*

- projects where the customer requires complete or significant control over the specification and service delivery, with little or no flexibility for the provider to propose new ways of doing things;

- contracts where there is little or no scope for continuous improvement;

- contracts where the customer requires an outcome, but cannot transfer key elements of control or major risks to the provider.

Rather than focusing solely on the benefits, costs and risks to the customer, partnering seeks to create a 'win-win' relationship, where both sides feel that the investments and concessions they have made, and the risks they have taken on, have helped them realize genuine benefits and achieve strategic goals.

Key features of the partnering approach

The key features of what the partnering approach is seeking to achieve must be set out in both the requirement and the formal contract – both partners must be clear about what they want and fully understand what is being proposed from the earliest stage and throughout procurement. Plans for how the risks will be managed must be made clear.

Traditional procurement concentrates on an examination of what the provider would do for the customer, with far fewer commitments in return; partnering focuses on what you could achieve together. Compromises may be required from either party and each should stress their organization's willingness to take a collaborative approach at all stages.

At the outset of the relationship, the customer's and supplier's objectives are unlikely to be aligned; incentives have to be designed to achieve this. Contracts that reward providers for helping deliver business objectives, but without attempting to transfer risks best managed by the customer, are an essential foundation for a good partnering arrangement.

Partnering principles

Partnering principles should guide both parties' actions throughout the procurement process and into contract management. There must be top management commitment from the start and throughout, from both parties. The right people need to be in place from the start who can build and maintain open relationships. As well as technical and business understanding, they will need to draw on abilities in communication, diplomacy and problem solving. They will need strong interpersonal skills, tact, patience, honesty and the ability to form strong professional relationships. A partnering approach takes time to plan so that the right people are in place from the start. You may need to consider how behaviours at many levels of the partnering organizations need to change in order to make partnering a success.

Figure 9.2 _continued_

Establishing and managing the relationship

Partnering arrangements mean differences in both corporate relationships and individual relationships. The way the two organizations regard each other is crucial, and above all else there must be mutual trust or the relationship may break down.

Trust needs to be developed – there will be little evidence of it on Day 1 although there will be plenty of good intentions. Trust has to be built and 'earned' through the right actions, behaviours and performance. There needs to be reality in the relationship and acceptance that there will be a steep learning curve. It is important to have the right people in the right place and this may require hard decisions about removing people who are hindering the relationship.

At the individual level, each one-on-one relationship should be peer-to-peer, with individuals chosen on the basis of their suitability for their role. At the management board level there should be mutual commitment.

A strong partnering arrangement starts with well-designed contractual clauses, but is then about establishing appropriate attitudes and behaviours. One of the key benefits of effective partnering is being able to raise issues or areas of concern at an earlier stage, thereby making them easier to re-solve. The roles, responsibilities, processes and mechanisms that will enable the relationship to grow and change need to be in place from the start.

Partnership mechanisms

■ **Partnering agreement**

This is usually created as a 'charter' to complement the formal contract terms. A partnering facilitator leads a workshop that helps both parties together to set out the principles, attitudes and ideals that will characterize the arrangement. These could include the degree of openness, the spirit in which problems will be handled, the desired 'tone' of the relationship, principles for communication, the behaviours of staff and so on.

■ **Incentives**

Increased benefits and savings for the customer justify additional supplier profit; for both parties, there could be profit share in return for improved efficiency and so on.

■ **Shared risk register**

This ensures complete understanding for both parties about risks to imple-mentation and ongoing service delivery, and enables a joint approach to man-aging risks. Clarity of who is responsible for and manages which risks is also essential.

Figure 9.2 *continued*

■ **Open book accounting**

There could be open book accounting for both parties, together with other measures that continually evaluate and demonstrate value for money, not lowest price. Actual costs and agreed profit margins are made visible, while also creating an understanding of the customer's budgetary restrictions. The degree of 'openness' needs to be carefully considered at the outset.

■ **Collaborative performance management**

A constructive, collaborative approach to setting targets and (in particular) baselines can help to build awareness of what can and cannot be achieved.

■ **Defined roles for relationship management**

As well as nominating individuals or teams for service delivery management and contract management, both parties should create relationship management roles. Their job will be to keep the relationship open and constructive, identifying problems early and moving to solve or escalate them as necessary.

■ **Means of communication**

Formal and informal communications should focus on dealing with exceptions and resolving problems together, promptly. For example, when a problem occurs each party could be required to explain the issues from the perspective of the other party. Staff from both parties should be involved where key business decisions are taken that affect the relationship and service delivery, especially where innovation is a key feature.

■ **Organizational learning and sharing knowledge**

It is important to ensure that lessons learned stay learned, and are passed on to others. Continuity of staff can preserve corporate memory; there should also be the means for embedding learning from the arrangement into future working practices and attitudes.

Common pitfalls

The wrong people

Choosing the wrong individual for a crucial role could derail the whole arrangement. In some situations, interpersonal skills could be more important than technical understanding.

Lack of cultural readiness

All the people in both the customer and supplier organizations who will be involved must be ready to make partnering work. Although the benefits of partnering may be clear and achievable, the organization may not be ready to work in new ways, or to be able to change in a short time.

Figure 9.2 _continued_

Unclear objectives

If the objectives of the arrangement for both parties are not clear at the outset, no amount of management effort will make the partnering relationship successful.

Inadequate performance measurement

The level at which services are currently provided, or the baseline from which improvements can be measured, are crucial to the way in which providers' performance will be assessed but can be very difficult to establish at the outset. In addition, finding relevant benchmarking measures that make meaningful comparisons between providers or suppliers can be hard to achieve.

Extracted and adapted from *Effective partnering; an overview for customers and providers*, published in March 2004 by the Office of Government Commerce as part of its Successful Delivery Toolkit.

Figure 9.2 *continued*

Index

Also by Harold Lewis:

Bids, Tenders & Proposals
Winning business through best practice

Whether you are engaged in professional services, consultancy or research, knowing how to write a winning tender is an essential business skill. To defeat the competition, you need to demonstrate value through every aspect of the tender and communicate it emphatically and irresistibly.

This unique book will enable you to do just that. It provides essential guidance on how to win services and consultancy contracts, research awards and government funding through competitive bids, tenders and proposals. Written in a crisp, accessible style using examples and detailed checklists, it explains how to create bids that are outstanding in both technical quality and value for money.

Harold Lewis writes from a background of specialist expertise in proposal writing and tender development. His book starts by highlighting aspects of bidding in three key areas:

- public sector procurement (particularly within the EU framework);
- contracts for private sector clients;
- applications for research funding.

Then the whole process of tendering is dealt with step by step, from the decision to put in a bid, through the task of managing its preparation and development, to the final stages of submission and evaluation.

Based on examples from actual winning tenders, *Bids, Tenders & Proposals* neatly combines a highly practical approach with a breathtaking breadth of scope. No other book covers the process of tendering in such business-like detail.

The above title is available from all good bookshops. To obtain further information, please contact the publisher at the address below:

Kogan Page Limited
120 Pentonville Road
London N1 9JN
United Kingdom
Tel: +44 (0) 20 7278 0433
Fax: +44 (0) 20 7837 6348
www.kogan-page.co.uk